Spiritual Healing

MIND · BODY · AND SPIRIT ·

Martin Daulby
and
Caroline Mathison

KT-153-795

LUCEAT LIBRIS DISSEMINAMUR

GEDDES&
GROSSET

This edition published by Geddes & Grosset, an imprint of
Children's Leisure Products Limited

© 1996 Children's Leisure Products Limited,
David Dale House, New Lanark ML11 9DJ, Scotland

First published 1996
Reprinted 1998, 1999

Cover photograph by Michel Tcherevkoff courtesy of
the Image Bank

ISBN 1 85534 378 9

Printed and bound in the UK

Contents

Introduction

Today's society stands as a multimedia monument to the scientific and technological triumphs of the past century. The radio crackled into life, man walked on the moon, and diseases that previously ravaged entire populations, such as tuberculosis and smallpox, were virtually eradicated overnight. Nowadays we can communicate through cyberspace, genetically engineer outsize fruit, and line up to be treated with the latest wonder-drug.

There is no denying that the advancements of science have made our lives infinitely easier, longer and more comfortable. We wonder how past generations can have possibly survived without mobile phones and watches that can withstand the pressure of thousands of fathoms of water.

Somewhere down the line science replaced religion and philosophy as the perceived source of infinite knowledge. Even the mysteries of creation, previously the domain of the divine, could be explained away in scientific terms.

In recent years, however, society has begun to doubt the omnipotence of science, realising that it cannot provide answers for some of the most fundamental questions of existence. From this realisation a new spirituality has emerged, which is heralding a gradual shift in attitude. The materialism and high-powered competitiveness of the 1980s has given way to a slightly more relaxed, positive and intuitive mood that has so far characterised the 1990s.

In no other arena has this generational shift been more apparent than in attitudes towards health. More and more people, doctors and patients alike, are adopting a more holistic approach to health, acknowledging the importance of lifestyle, proper diet and regular exercise in the upkeep of a healthy body. Even more importantly, people are beginning to recognise and understand the significance of the state of their mental, spiritual and emotional wellbeing on their physical health.

In reality, we have always known how strongly our emotions affect our physical being – think how many times dealing with someone difficult and demanding has brought on a headache. Even without realising it, we connect the idea of wellness with the idea of emotion when we say that we do not 'feel well', when we do not know specifically what is wrong with us. We also acknowledge our spiritual nature when we claim to be in 'high' or 'low' spirits.

It is in this atmosphere of renewed enthusiasm for the holistic ideal, however, that such concepts have been widely accepted into our collective consciousness. This in itself has paved the way for numerous alternative therapies, some of which have been practised for centuries either in other cultures or our own, to be adopted further into mainstream society. A whole world of esoteric therapies has become more socially acceptable as well as more readily available. Faith healing is just one of these therapies.

Some people feel uneasy about the term 'faith healing'. To many it positively smacks of jiggery-pokery, probably because of recent publicity about fraudulent American television evangelists, as well as a deeper-rooted fear and suspicion of anything that sounds vaguely occultist.

In fact, faith healing is one of the most conservative and respectable of all the battery of so-
called alternative therapies, being wholeheartedly
welcomed into institutions such as churches and
hospitals, as it is.

We should perhaps attempt at the outset to fash-
ion some working definition of faith healing. This
may be an elusive task because the term is such a
wide one, offering itself to various differing
schools. It should be pointed out that faith healing
has become an umbrella term for the diverse
strands of healing that fall within its range. In its
purest meaning, faith healing is the belief in
'right' thinking, practised within a religious system. Christian faith healers believe that all healing comes from God.

The term is really unsatisfactory because it implies that faith is the obligatory prerequisite to being helped by the healing forces. This excludes
many nonbelievers, who have been some of the
most startling subjects and benefactors of healing.
Another problem for some people with the term
'faith healing' is that it places the source of healing in a person's faith, not in Christ or a divinity.
Apart from belittling the role of God in healing,

this definition is also potentially harmful for those who do not experience any alleviation of symptoms following healing, leading them to believe that it is their fault for not having enough faith, which can result in a spiritual crisis.

A more flexible definition of faith healing is that of a therapy based on something other than current scientific knowledge. The term 'spiritual healing' is employed by those who are reluctant to be emphatic as to the origins of healing, be it from God or some other universal source. In this book the terms 'faith' and 'spiritual' healing are somewhat interchangeable, although Chapter 6 focuses specifically on 'spiritual healing' as distinct from 'faith healing'.

The word 'healing' comes from the Anglo-Saxon word 'healan', which connotes both the body and the spiritual element of the human being as the thing to be healed.

At this point, it would be politic to draw attention to the difference between healing and curing because they are *not* the same thing. Although it is true that miraculous cures do take place following faith healing, this is not the premise of the therapy. Healing could involve the temporary or permanent alleviation of symptoms, or it could mean reaching a state of wellbeing. On the other hand, the healing could just be arriving at a point of acceptance.

Redefining healing also means changing attitudes towards disease. It has been suggested that perhaps all diseases are psychologically rooted or stress-related. Some healers believe that all symptoms of disease are the result of some deeper spiritual disorder, and that the patient must subsequently look at his or her life and assess what it is that is making him or her unwell. For example, stress, over-work and unexpressed anger are widely recognised as contributing factors in the emergence of many medical conditions, ranging from migraines to cancer. This kind of direct cause and effect approach can be harmful, however, as it may suggest to the patient that he or she is somehow responsible for the illness. This could induce feelings of guilt and shame, both extremely negative emotions, which would become another barrier to wellbeing. By all means analyse your lifestyle in order to understand the possible origins of an ailment, just do not hold yourself to account.

It should also be emphasised that faith healing is

a complementary therapy intended to be employed in conjunction with orthodox medicine, *not* to replace it.

The proof of the effectiveness of this type of healing is anecdotal rather than scientific, which invites scepticism. In any analysis of faith healing we must accept that there are things in life that defy scientific explanation. As Shakespeare says through Hamlet, 'There are more things in heaven and earth, [Horatio], than are dreamt of in your philosophy'. Surely it is not beyond us to admit that our own knowledge may be flawed and imperfect.

It would be a tragedy indeed if we allowed our fear and mistrust of the unknown to deter us from embracing all that faith healing has to offer. With this in mind let us explore spiritual healing and its many possibilities.

Chapter 1

The Healing Tradition

Whence came faith healing? The practice has been prevalent in virtually all cultures and religious customs through the ages. Primitive peoples required a shaman, or medicine man, to cure their ills. The Ancient Greeks and Romans erected temples to Asclepius, the god of medicine. In the Judaic scriptures paranormal cures such as the answer to Abraham's prayer against barrenness and those of leprosy by Elisha and Moses are much in evidence.

Unorthodox healing – that is, the cure or assuagement of bodily or mental ills by supplication or religious rituals, which may either augment or replace medical care – includes fringe medicine, faith healing, spiritual healing and miracle cures.

Along with this diversity of schools, there is a correspondent diversity of opinions expressed about it. To its detractors it is merely superstition and quackery, practised by metaphysical 'wide boys' out for a fast buck. To its adherents it is an alternative perspective on the way we think of illness, the basic truth of which has yet to be accepted or assimilated into medical practice. Faith healing can also boast a rich and fascinating history, one replete with spirit and humour. It would be a mean soul that could not laugh at the enterprising Edinburgh quack James Graham, selling his celestial bed in a valiant attempt to emulate the great Cagliostro, a charlatan who practised alchemy and mysticism as the means to realise cures at the time of Louis XVI. Graham sold beds that he professed could provide painless childbirth, along with chairs that alleviated rheumatism, and for the noblemen that could pay for it, he could provide the elixir of life. Then there is the sheer romanticism and lust for life of a figure like Grigori Rasputin, leaving his wife and children to roam rural Russia as a faith healer after a strange religious revelation.

The revival of interest in faith healing is no

doubt due in some part to the New Age movement. This theorises that humankind is entering the Age of Aquarius and that we are due for a worldwide spiritual renewal. Part of the agenda of New Ageism is a preoccupation with complementary medicine, green issues, and interest in occultist and spiritualist practices. What is important to remember, however, is that this resurgence of interest in complementary therapy is nothing new – it occurs at regular intervals, a healthy antidote to the almost totalitarian stranglehold that the established medical world has on the way we perceive the concept of health and therapy. It will be no shock to learn that pre-Civil War America was just as infatuated with complementary medicine, albeit in a slightly different incarnation, as modern America is today. Perhaps the last British wave of this occurred in Georgian England, among fashionable society. No doubt New Ageism will not be the last of these flirtations with underground medicine.

New Age healing

The resurgence of interest in healing at present must be due in some part to the New Age movement, although the kind of healing prescribed by New Agers has more in common with Jungian psychology than with healing practised down the centuries. New Age healing consists of what is termed 'healing of the memories', 'healing emotional hurts', or 'soul healing'. The main idea behind this is that what is to be healed are negative past experiences rather than the physical body. These ideas were developed principally by Agnes Sanford and Morton Kelsey, although the influence of both Jungian and Freudian psychology hang heavily over the proceedings. The movement borrows heavily from Freud's idea of depth psychology, whereby one's childhood experiences are plundered for traumas and upset, which must then be confronted and healed.

Jungian psychology is also utilised, in that New Age healing encourages you to visualise Jesus accompanying you during the traumatic event of the past. This visualisation of the past with Jesus as a companion also extends to visualising the desired state you wish to reach through the healing process. The effect this has on the subconscious is supposedly meant to bring about what is wished for. As with Christian Science, many of the New

Age doctrines oppose and eschew traditional Christian ideas.

Of course, there is the darker side of faith healing, or rather the abuse of faith healing. There can be no whitewash of this in any respectable assessment of the topic. The excesses of the Eddy movement are unrelated to the issue of the validity of healing. Again, I have avoided elaborating on the moral bankruptcy of the Elmer Gantry breed of televangelist faith healer, not because I regard it as insignificant but because it deflects us again from asking the real questions – the question of the validity or otherwise of healing in the war on disease.

Before we can proceed, we have to accept that there really is something to be studied, abandon our prejudices and preconceptions, and set out with an open mind, something that is harder to do than we would often care to admit.

Healers and healing past and present

We shall endeavour here to provide a brief narrative of the history and personalities of faith healing through the centuries, with an awareness that we will ultimately fail because of the huge expanse of the subject. What we do hope to provide is an entertaining jaunt through this account of healing without being too dry or scholastic.

Faith healing was the dominant form of treatment five hundred years before Christ, concurrent with the time that hygienic therapy began among the Greeks. (Hygienic therapy advocates manipulation of the environment that sufferers inhabit to help them recover. Rest, fresh air and diet are its principal weapons against disease.)

Gradually drug cures became popular, and this was integrated into the usual faith healing practices. When Christianity began to make its influence felt, these drug cures were forced out, and once again pure faith healing became predominant and maintained its ascendancy for thirteen centuries. At the time of the Renaissance, faith healing began to lose its virtual monopoly on medical therapy but still had purchase in non-medical cults.

Pythagoras

Pythagoras, the sixth century BC astronomer, mathematician and physician, considered healing to be the most elevated of pursuits and saw it as an integral part of his deliberation on ethics, mind and soul. He called the healing energy *pneuma*, which he theorised arose from a fire at the core of the universe, which gave human beings their animation and immortal soul. His adherents believed this *pneuma* could be perceptible in a lucent body and that this light was capable of curing illness. They believed that all matter is comprised of opposites that are in conflict and have to be in equilibrium in order to be in harmony.

Hippocrates

Hippocrates (460–377 BC) was born on the Greek Island of Kos into a family of priests and physicians. He was educated at a famous school in Kos and received medical training from his father and other medical practitioners. By the time he had moved to Athens he had acquired outstanding proficiency in the diagnosis, prognosis and treatment of disease. He kept detailed accounts of mumps, epilepsy, hysteria, arthritis and tuberculosis. Hippocrates argued that all illness, both mental and physical, was caused by natural factors, such as organic injury or an imbalance of body fluids. The Greeks, beginning with Thales, had a tendency to replace magico-religious explanations for things with naturalistic explanations.

Hippocrates is held to be the father of modern medicine, although Alcmaeon and Empodocles had challenged medical practices based on superstition and magic before him. Hippocrates laid the basis of modern scientific medicine in his writings, called the Hippocratic *Corpus*. He also created the basis of medical ethics embodied in the Hippocratic Oath.

Hippocrates believed that the body had self-healing mechanisms, and it was the physician's duty to aid these natural processes. The cures of Hippocrates involved proper diet, rest and fresh air.

Hippocrates recognised that the alleviation of some symptoms by the so-called 'laying on of hands' was accompanied by a sensation of warmth and tingling. He described the healing energy: 'the heat that oozes out of the hand, being applied to the sick, is highly salutary'. He postulated that just as 'health may be implanted in the sick by certain gestures, and by contact, as some diseases may be communicated from one to the other'.

He postulated his own notion of the 'healing energy', or *pneuma*, and called it the *vis medicae naturae*. He believed that the proper flow of the pneuma could be disrupted by malign influences, which disturbed the relationship between the individual and the cosmos.

Unlike Pythagoras, Hippocrates advanced the view that mind and body were separate. The Hippocratic system was codified by Galen in the second century AD, although Galen himself suspected that the efficacy of the healing temples that were employed in Ancient Rome relied on some form of mental manipulation.

The idea that mind and body were separate became the orthodoxy to hold sway for many centuries afterwards. A few lone voices, such as Plato's, spoke out against this idea: 'the great error of our day,' he wrote, 'is that physicians separate the soul from the body.'

Asclepius

Perhaps the cult of Asclepius, the Greek god of healing, demonstrates that in the early Graeco-Roman tradition, magic and medicine ran side by side in the battle against illness. It is not really clear whether Asclepius was a real historical fig-

ure or a mythical one. Outside the stream of early
rational medicine was a widespread popular belief in the powers of early miracle-working wiz-
ards such as Serapis and Apollonius of Tyana. It
was also believed that to sleep with the fourth
book of the Iliad under one's pillow at night ensured a cure for the quartan ague!

The Asclepeion at Pergamum is one of the best
preserved and most famous of the medical
establishments of the Graeco-Roman era, being
founded in the first half of the fourth century BC
by Archias, who had been healed by Asclepius at
Epidaurus. Archias had sprained himself while
out hunting and had met a fast cure under the
management of Asclepius. Archias was so impressed by the treatment he had received that he
'brought the God to Pergamum' in the founding
of a temple there. The oracle at Delphi had already proclaimed that Asclepius was a healer of
diseases. The tale of the growth of the cult of
Asclepius in Rome in the year 292 BC is told by
Livy.

Classical civilisation entrusted its patients to the
incubation cure, a treatment that arose from the
cult of Asclepius. The patient would pass a night

in the 'incubation temple' in the belief that the gods would cure them in a dream. After ritual purification, suppliants for aid slept in the basement, or *adyton*, of the temple at the end of a long tunnel. Here they hoped to dream the dreams on whose interpretation by the priests depended their future treatment and welfare. The playwright Aristophanes (408–388 BC) makes reference to this ritual cult in his play *Plutus*.

Cures at Pergamum

Nicanor, a lame man, was sitting by the temple when a young boy ran up to him and snatched away his crutches. Nicanor chased after the boy in hot pursuit and was cured. There is also the story of two women who became pregnant after their visit to the temple. Andromache, the wife of King Arybbas of Epirus, 'for the sake of offspring', slept in the temple and saw in a dream a handsome youth uncovered and disrobed her, the god touched her with his hand, whereupon a child was born to her. The second lady, Agameda of Ceoa, was also infertile and went to sleep in the temple whereupon she dreamt of a serpent lying on her belly. Five children were later born to her.'

The plausibility of the cures at Pergamun are striking, especially the cures of psychologically induced ailments, although the cures administered at other health centres, such as Epidaurus, are no less striking. One patient remained sceptical, however. 'When parchance my penis was hurt . . . I feared the surgeon's hands. I was reluctant to entrust my membrum virile to the care and the very great gods such as Phoebus and the son of Phoebus.'

Much of Greek thinking on medicine was appropriated by the Romans, who then developed the idea of a public hospital system. But after the collapse of the Roman Empire there was a virtually complete return to magic and mysticism.

Paracelsus

Practising in the sixteenth century, Philippus Paracelsus (1493–1541) is regarded as the father of modern therapeutics. Leaving his native Switzerland after becoming unhappy with the means of procuring wisdom in his indigenous country, he travelled around Europe. Something of an unorthodox healer, during his travels he became acquainted with physic not in common use among doctors of medicine and accomplished many miraculous cures, acquiring a great reputation in the process.

Paracelsus developed the idea that human beings were an integral part of nature, suggesting that they were continuous with nature and reflected internally the broader cosmos in the external world. He claimed that healing energies existed and radiated in and around humans. He called this force *Archaeus*. This force was an ambivalent one because it could cause as well as cure disease. It was also contained, he argued, in stars and also in magnets. The notion of magnetism, as expounded by Mesmer, has its roots in Paracelsus. He also believed that negative thoughts could block the flow of *Archaeus* and result in illness. For most of his life he was regarded as a charlatan, but he massively enriched science in the course of his life, primarily in the fields of chemistry and medicine. He died at the hospital of St Sebastian at Salzburg in 1541.

Valentine Greatrakes and 'the king's evil'

'The king's evil' was the name sometimes given

to tuberculosis involvement of the lymph glands, formerly called scrofula. In fact, the term 'king's evil' came to be used for ailments other than scrofula, including a wide variety of complaints affecting the head, neck and eyes, especially swollen lips, tumours, sores and blisters. The disease had hideously disfiguring effects on the face and the body, and was widespread in the seventeenth century. It was so called because it was believed that the monarch had special powers of healing this disease, provided by the doctrine of the divine right of kings, a practice that began with the Anglo-Saxon king, Edward the Confessor, in the tenth century. The healing ability was called 'thaumaturgic', or miraculous. Under the Plantagenets, the royal touch swiftly became a vital attribute of kingship. Edward I (1272–1307) touched over a thousand people a year for the king's evil, and the practice was equally popular with his successors, Edward II and Edward III.

The healing benediction

Under the Tudors and Stuarts, the royal touch became increasingly popular, and elaborate ceremony was associated with it. After prayer, the king would touch the sufferer with his hand and then give him a coin. Originally, this coin would be silver, but by the time of Henry VII it had been replaced by gold. By the time of Charles I the coins themselves were thought to have healing powers.

We even have Shakespeare in social historian mode to describe the royal touch in *Macbeth*. The laying on of hands is referred to in these lines spoken by Malcolm, who is here describing the act of touching to combat the king's evil:

> How he solicits heaven,
> Himself best knows; but strangely visited people,
> All swoln and ulcerous, pitiful to the eye,
> The mere despair of surgery, he cures,
> Hanging a golden stamp about their necks,
> Put on with holy prayers; and 'tis spoken,
> To the succeeding royalty he leaves
> The healing benediction.

(Act 4, scene 3, line 149)

The practice of royal healing reached its height at the end of the seventeenth century. In France

Louis XVI gave the touch to a crowd approaching two thousand strong on one Easter Sunday. In England at around the same time, Charles II was giving the royal touch to five thousand sufferers a year.

The rise of the Stroker

Some may feel that there is an inherent irony in the idea of a Puritan faith healer, as the Puritan regards the physical body to be junk. But so it was that perhaps the greatest British healer of all arose from the ranks of the New Model Army.

Valentine Greatrakes was born in 1628 of English parentage and was thirty-four before he felt the impulse, the 'strange persuasion', that he had healing powers. At the beginning of the Irish Rebellion in 1641, he joined Cromwell's army as a cavalry lieutenant in Ireland. He was a wealthy man with an estate in Lismore, County Waterford. Cromwell banished Charles I, refusing to countenance his kingship or the purported power of the royal touch.

Because the royal touch was not available during the Commonwealth interregnum (Cromwell had tried and failed to administer it himself),

Greatrakes was seised with the conviction that
God had ordained that it was he who was blessed
with the gift of 'curing the King's Evil, which for
the extra ordinariness thereof, I thought fit to conceal for some time'. Greatrakes, or the 'Stroker'
as he came to be known (Greatrakes moved his
hands in a stroking motion without actually
touching the sufferer's body), was called a 'charlatan' in contemporary accounts, and even his
own wife was deeply sceptical of his healing
powers, calling them the result of 'idle imagination'. His wife's job was in the charitable dispensing of medicine to the poor, and this gave him the
perfect opportunity to test his powers, imaginary
or not.

An ecclesiastic who witnessed Greatrakes at
work ventured that what was happening was
'more than ordinary' but that it was 'not miraculous'. Some of the alleged 'healings' would last as
long as six weeks. The charge of charlatan was
perhaps unfair because Greatrakes himself was as
mystified by his own success rate as everybody
else. All he would offer was an intimation that
some form of exorcism was involved. He was also
a man of independent means and did not attempt

to charge his patients. Neither did he claim to be infallible; there were those that claimed that their pains returned after their supposed cures. One of his most famous failures was that of the first royal astronomer of England, John Flamsteed.

Greatrakes would originally treat maladies connected with the bones, and after a period of success that lasted two years he had developed enough confidence to believe that he could also treat agues, an intermittent fever with hot and cold sweats. The extension of his services was fuelled by the coming of various dreams, the import of which was that he should begin and then extend his ministry. His method was to direct the ailment by squeezing it to an extremity of the body where it could be isolated and then ejected. His fame and success were so great that he was forced to build an extension to his house to accommodate sufferers awaiting treatment. His fame spread to London, causing huge shiploads of sufferers to cross the Irish sea in the hope of an audience with the Stroker.

In 1666 Greatrakes travelled to London, where he exhibited his healing powers and met the famous of the day, who included the poet Andrew

Marvell and the chemist Robert Boyle. Boyle was to investigate Greatrakes's powers and find in favour of them. In 1667 Greatrakes's powers began to recede to nothing. Fewer and fewer patients came to visit him, his curative powers were no longer news, and the Stroker went into retirement.

Johann Joseph Gassner

Born in Austria, Gassner (1727–79) had a Jesuit education and was ordained as a Roman Catholic priest. He was the victim of illnesses such as headaches, gastric complaints and chest pains, illnesses that he would feel intensify as he gave Mass. He concluded that this was indeed none other than the devil trying to take possession of him.

His answer to this was to style a form of self-exorcism by which he found he could successfully alleviate these aches and pains. From the success of his self-diagnosis and treatment he began to shape the idea that a large proportion of human illness – with some exceptions – was due to diabolic influence.

When Gassner was nearing fifty he started to experiment, using his techniques on others who were suffering mental disturbance. This was so successful that as many as two thousand people a month were administered to at one of Gassner's mass healing ceremonies. Gassner employed a truncated form of exorcism, which departed from the standard ritual of bell, book and candle, a methodology that was to scandalise the church of the day. He had a powerful patron in the Bishop of Regensburg, yet this did not prevent the church's usual perfunctory dismissal of the Austrian healer. With Gassner's growing success, the demand for a convincing rebuttal of his practices from the established church became great. The church was also disgruntled by his eclectic approach to the healing ceremony. At one mass meeting at Ellwangen, Gassner amalgamated Roman Catholic ritual with evangelical showmanship and a personal idiosyncratic lingot of possession. It was witnessed that he would give a command in Latin to a patient to fall to the ground, and this would be followed, even though the patient knew no Latin. His patients would be seen to weep, become belligerent, and fall into trances.

Although his ability to achieve a form of mass hysteria is well documented, his ability to cure permanently was not so solid. The only certain cures he could convincingly claim were cures of rheumatic complaints. Eventually the end of Gassner's ministry came when the church forbade him to practise.

Maximillian Hehl was professor of astronomy at Vienna University and assigned himself the task of attempting to explain the cures and hysteria that Gassner had brought about. In doing so he came into contact and influenced the next key figure in healing – Friedrich Anton Mesmer.

Franz Mesmer

Friedrich Anton (Franz) Mesmer (1734–1815) appeared in Vienna at the end of the eighteenth century. He was born near Lake Konstanz, at Iznang in Swabia, a gamekeeper's son. Unusually for a healer, he qualified as a physician and gained four doctorates. In Vienna, he met a Jesuit priest called Maximillian Hehl, the same eccentric astronomer with an interest in the paranormal who had tried to study the method of Gassner. Through him Mesmer developed his interest in astronomy. Hehl told Mesmer of the cures he had brought about using a magnet. Mesmer himself then copied this method to try to cure one of his patients, where all other forms of treatment had failed. Tellingly, the success of the treatment on this and further patients always involved Mesmer telling his patient what exactly was expected to occur.

He developed a large practice, married a wealthy widow and lived in an impressive house on the Danube. His salon was frequented by such illustrious company as Haydn, Mozart and Gluck.

It was at this point that he began to develop his ideas on what he chose to call 'animal magnetism'. It was Mesmer who managed to draw attention to the notion of mental healing as distinct from religion. He substituted the notion of animal magnetism for religion in his practices, and after studying the techniques of Gassner, as Hehl had done before him, Mesmer came to the conclusion that he had stumbled on the same method that Gassner had utilised. He demonstrated his use of magnetic passes around the body in the treatment of illness. The passes first of all provoke a crisis: 'an attempt by nature to resist the illness' in Mesmer's words. This would manifest itself as hysteria in the patient. This technique is now better known as catharsis, a technique appropriated later by Sigmund Freud and Bleule. Mesmer at first employed magnets to this end, but later he discovered that his treatment was just as effective without their use. The person whose repute or personal charisma can induce the mental condition of concentration, obeisance, and positive expectation can presently disregard the application of passes and magnets and oil, as Mesmer did.

When magnetic therapy became popular, Hehl claimed to have been the first to use it. This led to a dispute between Hehl and Mesmer, which Mesmer won, perhaps unfairly.

He postulated that he injected a magnetic fluid into the patient. He inspired a faithful coterie but failed to be accepted by the medical establishment. He also advanced the idea that a psychic ether pervades space. This ether is then subject to tides that are caused by heavenly bodies. These tides run through all organic bodies, i.e. humankind. The free passage of these tides in the body is responsible for good health. Conversely, their blockage leads to ill health.

Although his salon was popular among the rich and fashion-conscious Viennese, an eighteen-year-old patient of Mesmer's, called Maria

Paradies, managed to provoke a scandal by claiming to have fallen in love with him after he allegedly restored her sight. Mesmer was forced to leave Vienna, ostensibly because he was a fraud. Mesmer's arrival in Paris in 1778 caused a sensation. Waving his hands over his patients' faces and gazing deeply into their eyes, he would 'mesmerise' them with an iron rod and put them into a deep trance. He had now taken to administering his treatment to groups rather than lone individuals, realising the power of collective psychology that could be activated in his treatments. Indeed, he called this the 'contagion effect'. He would also increase the use of ritual in his treatment, placing his patients in a dimly lit room and entering wearing a lilac cloak and waving a yellow wand.

He was also to find a receptive audience in Paris with Empress Marie Theresa of Austria's daughter, Marie Antionette, who became a disciple and Mesmer's patron. She offered Mesmer a chateau and a lifetime pension if he would disclose the secrets of his success. He declined. What Mesmer really wanted was acceptance from the medical profession.

Mesmer offered to submit his powers to the tests of the medical profession but was rebuffed. Eventually, a commission was set up in August 1784 in France to study Mesmer's success, which took an unenthusiastic view of his abilities and thereby marginalised him. The commission concluded that while many of Mesmer's abilities could be well substantiated, his success was due not to animal magnetism but to the suggestibility of his patients. The commission branded Mesmer a fanatic and a mystic, and admittedly some of his patients were observed to be badly affected by Mesmer's methods. Yet he still managed to make a considerable fortune from his practices. He died at the age of eighty in Switzerland.

Emil Coue

In Nancy, France, in the 1880s, the French healer Emil Coue studied mesmerism and became intrigued with the idea that a mysterious energy called animal magnetism flowed between the healer and the patient. Coue was a chemist, a man of science, and cynical about healing, so much so that he began to conduct experiments that attempted to unseat the popular belief in mesmerism. These experiments were conducted by selecting a group of patients being treated conventionally and dispensing to them bottles of coloured water of no medicinal value. The patients believed that this water was a new wonder-drug. He found that those who were given the coloured water recovered more successfully than those who followed the doctor's prescribed course of drugs. Coue concluded that it was not mesmerism but suggestion that had cured them.

He developed from this his theory of autosuggestion, which entailed that all his patients had to do was to believe that their illnesses could be counteracted simply by believing with all their heart that the illness they suffered would vanish. He implored his patients to say to themselves the slogan, 'Every day, in every way, I get better and better.'

Zouave Jacob

A Frenchman born in 1828, Jacob served as a trombonist in the military band of the Zouaves. His gift of healing was first noticed when he served in the Crimea and Algeria, but it first came to public attention when a national paper pub-

lished articles on his healing ability while he was
serving in Châlons. When his fame began to grow,
the public would flood to his tent and disrupt the
work he was alloted. A transfer to Versailles
landed him a rich patron in Paris. Jacob was dis-
charged from the army at the age of thirty-nine,
when the same crowds that had pursued him in
Châlons followed him to Paris. Like Greatrakes,
Jacob had no explanation for his abilities and was
not an especially religious person. He believed
that his powers were not supernatural in origin.
He claimed that he could cure 'all kinds of diseases' but that he was not regularly victorious
over any one disease. Also in his favour was the
refusal to accept money for his abilities, even
when it was stipulated it should go to the poor.
One friend described him as 'a most intractable,
disagreeable fellow'. Jacob was no charmer, so
any idea that his popularity spread because of personal charisma can be dismissed at once. After
one healing session, a group of the healed moved
to thank him for his attention, but Jacob was seen
to dismiss them 'brutally', as one commentator
observed.

His methodology included touch and command

as well as staring deep into the patient's eyes – a journalist described his 'trancelike carriage' and the intensity of his eyes, from which 'intense light shot out'. He would also stipulate that the patient should be in his presence. Sometimes his command to walk would be punctuated by him stamping his foot on the floor with 'rude violence'. Jacob could diagnose the ailment of a patient almost immediately on sight and was, as far as we can tell, always right. At the height of his powers, he could bring a roomful of cripples to walk with the command 'arise and be well'.

Eventually the combined antagonism from both the clerical and medical professions led to a falling off in popularity for Jacob. He continued to heal up to his death in 1914, but his glory days were gone.

Grigori Rasputin

The most notorious faith healer in Russian history was the debauchee Grigori Rasputin. Born in an obscure Siberian village, he was the third and last child of Efim Akovlevich, a well-to-do farmer. As well as the gift of healing, he was reputed to be blessed with clairvoyance, as a child being able to detect any missing object in the house and to sniff out the local thieves in his community. As a child he would also hear the stories of the pilgrims that passed through his town, exciting him and imbuing him with a sense of the religious at an early age. At twenty, he married a local girl, Praskovia Feodorovna, and fathered four children.

According to his daughter, a chance frolic with three Siberian peasant girls in a lake led to a religious revelation, and soon afterwards, in approximately 1900, he joined a maverick religious sect, called the Khlist, who openly advocated sexual indulgence in their philosophy. They were flagellents who believed that man must at first sin in order to be redeemed later, so Rasputin set about sinning in his own inimitable way. Rasputin proved to have such a natural aptitude for this that he was exiled from his own village by the local priests and so began an odyssey of itinerant wandering through rustic Russia, performing cures and initiating thousands of women into flagellation.

Rasputin had an uncanny ability to calm the troubled minds of those who surrounded him. As well as this, he had a virtually unerring ability to assess the strengths and weaknesses of character in his contemporaries, an ability that was eventually to be utilised by the Tsarina herself.

By 1905 he had settled in St Petersburg, where tales of his amazing healing powers had reached the ear of both Tsar Nicholas II and Tsarina Alexandra. One of the most famous healings that Rasputin administered was to one of his own disciples, Olga Lokhtina. Olga was to be the first of Grigori's upper-class friends. Rasputin purportedly cured her of a nervous stomach disorder, called neurasthenia, that she had been plagued with for five years. In this cure Rasputin used both impassioned prayer and hypnotic suggestion, convincing Olga that he was in league with the Almighty in assuaging the illness.

He rose to become a close confidante of Tsarina Alexandra, mainly because of his ability through hypnosis to help her sick son, Alexis, who was afflicted with haemophilia. The child of Lili Dehn, the Tsarina's lady in waiting, was also cured of a fever by Rasputin after heartfelt prayer. By the end of 1906 he had established a firm reputation as a healer.

Rasputin also gave the Tsar and his wife a feeling of being in touch with the real Russia of the peasants. The notion that true faith was more likely to be found among the people was common, and no doubt this contributed to the allure Rasputin held for the Tsarina. He would assure them that Russia loved the Tsar. Correspondingly, the Assyrian healer Mrs Davitashvili has been quick to emulate this asset and pretends to a oneness with the people. She has said: 'It is every citizen's duty to inform the president of the people's views.' Rasputin used the Tsarina's favour to protect himself and broaden his influence, even though his wild sexual antics were scandalising the whole of St Petersburg. In 1916, a gang of conservative noblemen, led by Felix Yusopov, assassinated him.

Felix Kersten: faith healing and the Third Reich

That the Nazi movement was deeply interested in the occult is no big surprise to anyone nowadays. Yet fewer people are aware that the presence of healing fell on the Third Reich. That a death cult should embrace a life cult is strange enough, but one of the strangest stories of all faith healing is that of the relationship between Heinrich Himmler and his personal healer, Felix Kersten. Kersten was born in 1898 in Finland, but spent most of his early life in the Netherlands and came to regard himself as Dutch. He became adept at massage, and extended his powers after meeting a mysterious oriental occultist called Ko. Through the tutelage of Ko, Kersten developed a method that allowed him to be able to diagnose ailments by means of that ancient technique, the laying on of hands. He could also, he discovered, transfer some of his own energy into the body of the recipient, in the manner of a spiritual healer. When he laid hands on the body of a patient he could feel his whole being flowing through the tips of his fingers into the patient. His ability to relieve pain began to be nothing short of miraculous, and even after the departure of Ko, his amazing powers remained.

His reputation began to grow, his practice prospered, and eventually he rose to such a pre-eminent position that he became the personal doctor of the Dutch royal family. This rise to sudden fame was not without its drawbacks, however. In 1938 he was asked to contact the head of the SS and high priest of the Nazi movement, Heinrich Himmler, with a view to assisting his stomach ailments.

Since Himmler's appointment as head of the SS, the stomach cramps from which he had periodically suffered from the beginning of the Nazi years had become so bad and unremitting that he was in a state of almost constant pain. The visits of doctors and the ministrations of orthodox medicine had done nothing to alleviate these pains, yet after a period of five minutes with Kersten, on his first timorous meeting with the head of the most feared organisation in the world, the pains had gone. Himmler was suitably impressed, and Kersten was appointed personal doctor. Kersten then became so invaluable to Himmler that the head of the SS could barely countenance the idea of being apart from him. Himmler was probably aware that Kersten's sympathies lay with the Jews but was too dependent on him to care.

After his appointment Kersten used his influence subtly to attempt to dissuade Himmler from his maniacal barbarities against the Jews. His first success was with his own native land. Himmler,

in July 1942, travelled to Finland to demand that
the Finnish Jews be handed over to Germany and
the political power of the Third Reich. In Finland
Kersten made contact with the Finnish foreign
minister and hit on a plan to stall the Nazi
operation. He persuaded Himmler that the Jewish
question was far too important to be decided by
anything less than parliament, which did not meet
for another four months, in November. It was
December before Himmler raised the issue again,
only to be dissuaded again by Kersten. The
Finnish Jews were saved.

This was only the first of many successes for
Kersten. He also managed, among other things, to
mastermind the release of concentration camp
prisoners to Sweden. His only failure was his attempt to persuade Himmler to make peace with
the Western Allies, after the attempted deposing
of Hitler.

Jose de Freitas – Arigo

Jose de Freitas, or 'Arigo' as he was affectionately known to his followers, astounded Brazil
through the 1950s by his use of so-called 'psychic
surgery'. He operated in completely insanitary

conditions and his tools were highly unorthodox –
table knives and scissors.

His ministry was begun with perhaps the strangest initiation rites in the history of faith healing.
He was present at the bedside of a dying woman,
who happened to be the wife of an acquaintance.
Suddenly, this unlettered ex-miner from
Conghonhas do Campo, with no instruction in
medicine, moved to grasp a nearby kitchen knife
and then, without further ado, plunged it straight
into the stomach of the woman. He then managed
to extract a huge tumour from the stomach, only
nearly to collapse after the realisation of what he
had done hit him. Later, a doctor found the tumour to have been a uterine tumour. Arigo
claimed no memory of the incident. The patient,
who had been considered near death, made a full
recovery and claimed to have felt no pain during
the involuntary operation.

A yet more bizarre twist in the story was to follow. In a trance Arigo revealed that a German
doctor, Adolphus Fritz (whose identity still remains unconfirmed), guided him in these unique
operations by speaking into his right ear while the
operations were conducted. Stranger still, Arigo

claimed Fritz had died in Estonia in 1918. To compound this, Arigo once broke into fluent German when speaking to the German husband of a patient, under the influence of Fritz.

Twice jailed by the Brazilian authorities despite the avowal and support of his devoted followers, first in 1956 and again in 1964, Arigo's fame spread, and the sick flooded to his small house in Conghonhas do Campo. In 1968 a team of doctors saw him treat over a thousand patients. They were led by the doctor Andrija Puharich, who was stirred by what he witnessed. He would watch Arigo stare solemnly at the patient and then make an impromptu diagnosis of his or her illness. This diagnosis would then invariably be found to be accurate by the team on investigation. After having told his friends that they would not see him again, he was found dead in a car crash.

Djuna Davitashvili

The former Soviet Union's best-known healer, Djuna Davitashvili, began her career as a qualified medical researcher before developing her 'information-energy interaction with living organisms', coupled with 'contact and non-contact' massage. Possessed of penetrating and hypnotic eyes, her amazing success rate has allowed her to build up her own busy clinic in Moscow.

At the time of the inception of this book, President Boris Yeltsin was reported to be consulting Davitashvili, who chanced to be the selfsame faith healer used by one of his predecessors, Leonid Brezhnev. The illness of Yeltsin now dictates that foreign observers adopt a wait and see approach rather than give willing assistance to reform. Yeltsin's use of the powers of Djuna Davitashvili is rich with irony, as Yeltsin was part of the team of Gorbachev supporters that mocked, for political ends, Brezhnev's use of faith healing.

Davitashvili calls herself a 'chaneller of bioenergy'. Davitashvili is Assyrian and a Russian monarchist – her love of nobility has lead her to emulate them, as she is known to be fond of giving out 'titles' to believers in her mystical powers. Djuna Davitashvili claims to be a regular visitor to the Soviet leader, boosting his 'bioenergy' and alleviating the weight of office with her technique of 'contactless massage'.

Djuna Davitashvili is also famed for her powers of diagnosis. She participated in tests for the

Washington Research Centre, which established that she could diagnose the various complaints of a group of forty-three subjects with a 97 per cent accuracy. She even went so far as to diagnose hitherto undetected complaints in the study group that were later substantiated by examination.

Perhaps we should not be so shocked at the use of healers by the Soviet premier as both Yeltsin and Brezhnev spent their formative years in an atmosphere of profound superstition and belief in folk medicine. It was the old Russia that retained its belief in faith cure and folk medicine long after the dominance of such practices weakened in Europe. It was only just over a century ago that every Russian village had a wizard, almost as a matter of course, and witches were hardly less prevalent. And of course one of the most famous faith healers of all time, and a creature of this very culture, Rasputin, died within living memory.

Chapter 2

Faith Healing and the Church

'And great multitudes came unto him, having with them those that were lame, blind, dumb, maimed, and many others, and cast them down at Jesus's feet; and he healed them; Insomuch that the multitude wondered, when they saw the dumb to speak, the maimed to be whole, the lame to walk, and the blind to see; and they glorified the God of Israel.'
(Matthew 15:30)

Healing was one of the most important ministries of a youthful church, which was fervent to evangelise and extend the Gospel of Jesus Christ. The notion of healing, for instance, is deeply embed-

ded in the Catholic liturgy. The sacraments of
penance and the anointing of the sick place healing firmly in the middle of the liturgical life of the
church. In the Maundy Thursday service, for instance, when the priest blesses the oil of the sick
he says: 'May your blessing come upon all who
are anointed with this oil that they may be freed
from pain, illness and disease and made well
again in body, mind and soul.' It is clear from this
that originally the anointing was intended as a
curative ritual, but this metamorphosed in the
Dark Ages into 'extreme unction', with the accent
on spiritual readiness for death because it had
proved so ineffective. Yet in the modern age the
logical implications of what really lies behind
these words is tactfully ignored. In Old English
texts, the word 'healand' could be used in place of
the word 'Jesus'.

For reasons we shall explore, however, the
place of healing has been torn from the heart of its
teaching and bulldozed to the sidelines. Eventually healing became a perfunctory practice within
the church, and this has remained the case up to
the present day.

The Christian religion has been systematically

denatured. There are millions of people in the world at this very moment who are needlessly suffering because the church has not adequately brought the healing message of Christ's ministry into the lives of its believers, and, indeed, its non-believers. How did this happen?

During the apostolic era of the church, healing was a common activity of the church, and this goes some way to explain the remarkable growth in popularity of what was, after all, a sect among sects. Some commentators have pointed out that the immense success of Christianity over other religious sects that were competing with it at the time of its inception was due to the fact that it was commonly believed that the early Christian church was the most capable and successful sect at the practice of healing. This means that the practice of faith healing is one of the cornerstones of our civilisation, as Western culture is a mixture of Christian and Hellenistic influences. The successful practice by the early Christians ensured that Christianity waxed while other religious sects waned.

Healing was looked upon as one of the most significant vocations of a nascent church that was ar-

dent to convert with the Gospel of Jesus Christ.
Thus it truly could be said that it was under the
aegis of faith healing that Christianity rose to
prominence.

The healing ministry of Jesus

'His reputation continued to grow, and large
crowds would gather to hear him and to have
their sickness cured, but he would always go off
to some place where he could be alone and
pray.'
(Luke 5:15–16)

Perhaps some readers may be offended that
Jesus should be discussed solely as a faith healer,
with the implication that he can be equated with a
huge panoply of faith healers, many of whom
were charlatans. Although it cannot be denied that
Jesus was the archetypal healer-priest figure embodied in the earlier traditions of Greece and
Egypt, it is instead our intention to show that faith
healing held a deeper significance to Christ's ministry and was used as a symbolic tool by Jesus in a
way that no other faith healer has ever approached
or contemplated.

For the Hebrews, the concept of healing someone entailed healing all that they were, and this attitude would have been shared by Christ himself. In fact, this is evidenced by Jesus's remark to a man who was lame. Jesus pointedly asked of him: 'Wilt thou be made whole?' (John 5:6). His question was concerned with the mental attitude of his patient as well as his physical condition. When Christ healed the paralytic, he first healed his soul, and then his body (Matthew 9:2–7). Neither the soul nor the body was prioritised.

Even a rudimentary scan of the Bible reveals that the ministry of Christ and faith healing are concepts that are inextricably linked. Christ is said to be responsible for fifty paranormal occurrences recorded in the Gospels, although many of them would be viewed as the casting out of spirits rather than faith healing.

Jesus faced opposition virtually as soon as he began his public ministry. After healing the sick and casting out many evil spirits, his family were scandalised enough that they went to take charge of him, for they said 'He is out of his mind' (Mark 3:21). Even his mother Mary went to Capernaum to take charge of Jesus.

Jesus employed healing by touch: 'Then he touched their eyes, saying "According to your faith be it unto you". And their eyes were opened.' This was the origin of the practice of kings to touch the afflicted to ward off the king's evil. Sometimes this theme was varied by using spittle. Jesus himself employed this method, part of the lore of the time.

Sometimes an order was employed by Jesus in the healing process: 'Rise, take up thy bed and walk'(John 5:6). Jesus was also aware of the cathartic effect of the removal of unconscious guilt feelings: 'Your sins are forgiven you.' According to the New Testament, Jesus Christ sometimes brought about physical cures through the forgiveness of sin (Matthew 9:2–7). The early Christians followed his example and prayed for the healing of the sick (James 5:14–16). A sacrament of healing, the anointing of the sick, developed in the Catholic tradition, and faith healing services have been part of the Protestant tradition also.

An interesting example can be found in the book of Mark, which tells of Jesus turning around in the crowd.

'Who touched my clothes?'

'You see the people crowding against you,' his disciples answered, 'and yet you can ask, "Who touched me?"'

But Jesus kept looking around to see who had done it.

(Mark 5:30–32 NIV)

Jesus also seemed to be able to radiate a healing power about him. On one occasion a woman who was suffering with a continual menstrual flow, and was, therefore, ceremonially unclean touched Jesus's garment unobserved, only to find him turn around and demand: 'Who touched my garment?' Jesus had felt the healing power be drawn from him, even though his attention was focused elsewhere. The story makes clear that it is her faith that cures her and not the magic of Jesus' robe, although at the time it was a widespread belief that cures could be brought about by touching a healer.

Christ would heal hundreds of sufferers until too exhausted to carry on. He also said that others were endowed with this ability: 'He who believes in me will also do the works that I do.'

More individual healings occur in the New Testament than in the Old. At the beginning of his public ministry, Jesus announced that the Kingdom of God was near (Mark 1:15) and immediately began healing the sick and casting out demons. Of the 3,774 verses in the four Gospels, 484 relate specifically to the healing of physical and mental illness and the resurrection of the dead. Of the 1,257 narrative verses in the Gospels, 484 verses are devoted to describing Jesus's healing miracles.

The last miracle that Christ wrought before the crucifixion, as documented in St Luke, was perhaps also one of the most wonderful and awe-inspiring:

'And a certain one of them smote the servant of the high priest and struck off his right ear. But Jesus answered and said, Suffer ye thus far. And he touched his ear and healed him.'

(Luke 22:50)

The ability to heal was given to the seventy-two disciples: 'Cure those who are sick and say, "The Kingdom of God is very near to you"' (Luke 10:9–10). Jesus promised to everyone who believed in him that 'he will perform the same works as I do myself' (John 14:12).

It was expected that in the early church the apostolate of healing would intensify. It is written that 'these will be the signs that will be associated with believers; they will lay their hands on the sick who will recover' (Mark 16:16–18).

If a layman was found to have the gift of healing it was considered to be a qualification for ordination.

In the first miracle after the Pentecost, Peter gave strength to a man of whom it was said that he had been 'lame from his mother's womb'. The apostle Paul saw a man at Lystra, who was thought to be 'a cripple from his mother's womb'. Paul implored the man in a loud voice to 'stand upright on thy feet', and thus the man rose to his feet. When Eutychus fell from the third storey and was 'taken up dead', Paul restored him to life again. Paul, when visiting the island of Melita, appeared to the people of the island holding a viper. When the people saw that Paul came to no harm in spite of this, they came to the conclusion that he was a god. Paul is then credited with healing the diseases of the whole island. Healing,

then, came to occupy the centre of the early
church's activities, with successful cures being
carried out by St Jerome.

The decline of healing

After the apostolic era of the church, a change in
emphasis on the significance of suffering occurred. Suffering began to be viewed as such a
blessing that it was wrong to seek healing. One
could perfectly imitate Christ by subjecting oneself to his suffering. Instead of healing, the church
began to highlight almost exclusively the spiritual
significance, and even worthiness, of suffering.
Suffering became a sign of predestination and immediate entry into heaven, because it was conjec-
tured that the sick did their suffering on earth. The
notion that suffering has an ultimate redemptive
value is still with us today.

In his early writings St Augustine argued that
healing was meant for the early church but Christians should not look for a continuance of healing.
Eventually he came to change his mind in his
book *Retractions*, and declared in it that he was
wrong. What had made him change his mind was
his experience as bishop of Hippo (*c*. 420 AD):

' . . . I realised how many miracles were occurring in our own day and which were so like the miracles of old . . . how wrong it would be to allow the memory of these marvels of divine power to perish from among our people . . . '

As the church began to consolidate its power, it became antagonistic towards pagan healing traditions until, by the Middle Ages, healing had become a renegade practice and the Catholic church warned its congregations that lay healers were in league with the devil. By the sixteenth century, in virtually all of Europe healing was banned.

Priests had been free to practise medicine right up to the thirteenth century, when a papal decree had disallowed the practice. The result of this was that religion and medicine went their separate ways. The church would attend to one's soul and the physician to one's body.

Philosophy played a prominent part in the fall of healing. As well as Descartes' divorcing of the mind and body, Spinoza (1632–77) managed comprehensively to unseat the church's belief in the miraculous by suggesting that God was the cause of everything and he acted in accordance with rigid inviolable laws. Rationalism was systematically to undermine the belief in the supernatural and, by extension, the reality of healing.

Healing in Britain

The position on healing in England in the sixteenth century was ambivalent. Healing was easily equated with witchcraft because of its mystery and invisible processes, but protection was offered to herbalists and other folk medicine practices. In the England of the sixteenth and seventeenth century, the customary reaction to illness was to probe one's individual soul for moral misdemeanours. Physical sickness was a theological issue, and this is clear in the Elizabethan Prayer Book's command to clergymen visiting the sick to remind their patients that the illness that had befallen them was of God's decree. The ancient link between the Christian view of illness as a curse from God exists in the names of certain illnesses – St Vitus dance and St Anthony's fire (Sydenham's chorea and ergotism respectively) are two examples.

In the England of the eighteenth century, healing was losing ground rapidly. Thomas Hobbes (1588–1679), the author of *Leviathan*, argued that the miracles enumerated in the Old Testament could not be given credence because if they had actually happened they would have automatically brought about a worldwide wholesale belief in the Christian religion.

The Age of Enlightenment brought about perhaps the severest critic of healing, David Hume. In his 1748 essay on miracles he argues that they are a 'violation of the laws of nature'. These laws were fixed and inviolable, and he would not tolerate the suggestion that they could be transcended.

In recent history a growing awareness of literary forms in the Bible by scripture scholars and theologians has led to some quarters questioning whether or not we should take the miracles of Christ in a literal way. Today people are more interested in the historical truth of the miracles, so that the miracle stories are interpreted as having a symbolic meaning rather than a literal one. There was admittedly an inclination to embellish healing stories and inflate the numbers involved. For instance, Mark (10:46) has one blind man whereas Matthew has two (20:30). It has also been observed that some miracles resemble Rabbinic stories and older legends. Furthermore, there is a description of Vespasian healing a blind man using saliva, and a myth in the cult of Dionysus describing water being turned into wine. The healing miracles in the Bible also follow the template of other miracle stories in the Gentile miracle story tradition.

Christian existentialists such as Husserl and Kierkegaard denied the supernatural as a reality. The German Lutheran theologian Rudolf Bultmann was also to deny the objective reality of Jesus's healings.

The only form of healing accepted by many churches is so-called 'spiritual' healing. If genuine physical healing takes place, it is regarded as a problem; the Catholic church tends to distance itself from healers who claim divine inspiration in case these healers should turn out to be charlatans. While this approach is no doubt politic, it tends to undermine the place of healing in religious life. As well as this, many Christians believe that the 'well of healing' dried up with the early church and limit the healing ministry of Christ to three short years of his life.

While it may be fashionable to query the literal truth of the healings of Jesus, whether we accept the healing miracles or not, we have to see the healing ministry of Christ as central to the life of Jesus Christ and his message. Healing was Christ's symbolic way of saying to his people that he understood their problems, and was not unaware of them.

Christ's whole existence was full of suffering, his death on the cross being only the culmination of his sufferings. The Hebrews whom Jesus dwelt amongst, and indeed ministered to, saw people in a holistic sense – that is, as a person with a body, a soul, feelings and a personal history. All these things had to be integrated into a harmonious unity of absolute concord in the healing process. Illness is not just a meaningless event but to a large extent the child of a person's fears, aspirations and actions. This is a central tenet of the philosophy of holism. Holism is a philosophy that may appear new but clearly is linked to the older tradition of Plato, the Hebrews and the Chinese, along with the Yogis.

Chapter 3

Lourdes – A Place
of Healing?

In the previous chapters of this book we have tended to concentrate on the personalities who have become well known as a result of their alleged powers of spiritual healing. Any book about faith healing, however, would not be complete without an examination of the places where many people claim to have been cured of debilitating illnesses after visiting the supposed place of healing. Medjugorje in Bosnia-Herzogovina, the Portuguese village of Fatima, and Knock in the Irish Republic are regarded as nothing less than holy shrines by thousands of people (Catholics and non-Catholics alike) who make their annual pilgrimage to these places. It is Lourdes, however, a

small town in the French Pyrenees, which, more
than any other shrine, has become synonymous
with faith healing. We will examine how Lourdes
became the place of worship that it is today, and
whether any authenticity can be attached to the
many recorded cases of miracle cures.

The story of St Bernadette

The story of Lourdes began in February 1858
when a fourteen-year-old peasant girl named
Bernadette Soubirous looked upwards and saw
what she considered to be an apparition of the Virgin Mary. Bernadette claimed that she beheld the
apparition a further seventeen times. Considering
that Lourdes today is held in such reverence by so
many pilgrims, it may surprise many that
Bernadette's claim to have seen the Virgin Mary
was initially met with great suspicion by many
people, including her parish priest, who went so
far as to accuse her of lying. Others more toler-
antly regarded her as a young girl with a fertile
imagination who craved attention, while others
were so hostile towards her that they physically
attacked her.

Bernadette began to refer to the vision as

'Aquero', which in local dialect meant 'that one'.
It was when Bernadette found the courage to talk
to the vision that she was told by the mysterious
'lady in white': 'I cannot promise happiness to
you in this world, only in the next.' During the
ninth apparition, Bernadette was told to search in
a muddy grotto, and it was here that she came
across a spring, the story quickly spreading
throughout the village that the water that flowed
from it would provide a miracle cure to people
who were afflicted by illness if they drank it. If
indeed Bernadette was a young girl who merely
craved attention, then she was certainly getting it
by now, with thousands of people from the village
and beyond gathering at the site of the alleged
miracle, hopeful that they would behold the Virgin Mary in front of them. Nonetheless, the whole
spectacle was still viewed with deep suspicion
and hostility by many. Her parish priest was as
sceptical as he was when she told him about the
first vision, and the commissioner of police regarded her as a nuisance, warning her not to make
any more visits to the spring. She was interviewed
by several people in authority, who were becoming increasingly concerned about the amount of

people who were congregating at the spring. During one of the last apparitions to take place, the figure told her that a shrine should be built at the place where the sightings occurred. The parish priest, when told of this by Bernadette, retorted that he would only believe such a story if a miracle occurred that could be witnessed by the mass of people gathered there, not just Bernadette. But although such an event would take place later, something happened that made the Roman Catholic authorities treat the matter seriously for the first time. On another visit to the spring, the white figure appeared to Bernadette again and told her that she was 'the Immaculate Conception'.

A week later, Bernadette went to the same spot where, by this time, crowds would regularly be gathering to pay homage. She carried a solitary candle and looked awestruck at what many now considered to be the Virgin Mary. Astonishingly, she felt no pain as the flame on the candle burnt downwards and dropped searing wax on her hands. Even more astonishing was the fact that there were no burn marks on her hands. These two occurrences finally convinced the parish priest that Bernadette was speaking the truth.

By now, pilgrims were arriving from all over the world, finally convinced that the apparition that appeared before Bernadette so many times was the Virgin Mary, and that it was her miraculous powers that caused the water to flow from the spring. Bernadette, now unable to lead a normal life, found sanctuary in the local nunnery, where she remained until her death in 1879 at the age of thirty-five. Bernadette was beatified in 1925 and canonised eight years later.

One final footnote is worth mentioning. Before her sanctification, the court of canonisation set up a commission, which entailed opening the sarcophagus, followed by exhumation and examination of the body. Considering that more than forty years had passed since Bernadette's death, the physicians were stunned at what they saw. Franz Werfel, in his book *The Song of Bernadette*, wrote that: 'Bernadette's girlish body showed no signs of corruption. It was almost unchanged. Face, hands and arms were white and their flesh soft. The mouth was a little open, as though breathing, so that the shimmer of the teeth was visible. The body itself was rigid and so firm that the nuns of Nevers, who witnessed the official exhumation, were able to lift it and deposit it unharmed in a new coffin, like that of one just dead.'

Miracles happen – don't they?

There have been so many recorded cases of alleged miracle cures at Lourdes that it is extremely difficult to ascertain how many of these cases are fallacies and how many are genuine. (Or at least how many pilgrims genuinely felt that their illnesses and disabilities were cured as a direct result of their visiting the shrine, even though their return to health may have been brought about by circumstances that owed nothing to divine intervention.)

It should be emphasised here that of the many thousands of pilgrims who have claimed that the healing powers of Lourdes have had a beneficial effect on them, fewer than a hundred have actually been recognised by the Roman Catholic church as being miraculous. This does not mean, however, that the Vatican has always been unerringly correct in its assumptions that miraculous healing powers have occurred or otherwise. The criteria for the authentication of supposed miracles have become increasingly stringent with the advancement of science and technology. This stringency has meant that there are doubtless several cases that, although regarded as genuine one hundred years ago, would not be viewed as such in the late twentieth century.

Before discussing whether the incidents of people being cured of illness and disease at Lourdes can really be assumed to be the result of miraculous and unearthly powers, we will recount some of the more well-known tales of pilgrims who have claimed that divine intervention has been largely responsible for them to lead a life free of illness.

John Traynor

The story of John Traynor, an Irishman born in 1883, is one of the most famous cases to be associated with Lourdes and its supposed healing powers. After being drafted into the Royal Navy in 1914, the ship on which he sailed was posted to Egypt, where he had at least two head wounds inflicted upon him. Furthermore, he suffered bullet wounds in his chest, with one bullet becoming lodged close to vital nerves in his shoulder, which rendered his right arm completely paralysed.

Traynor refused to heed the advice of surgeons, who urged him to agree to have his right arm amputated. Worse was to follow, however. He began to suffer epileptic fits, was unable to control his bodily functions, and by 1923 was a virtual paraplegic.

During this year, it came to his attention that an excursion was planned to Lourdes by the Liverpool diocese and, ignoring pleas from people who thought that the strain of the journey would kill him, he travelled with the rest of the pilgrims to France. It soon became apparent that the concern that his fellow travellers had displayed at the outset of the journey were being realised, for his condition deteriorated and he suffered another epileptic fit, and after being admitted to a Lourdes hospital, his epilepsy and paraplegia were officially recorded. It was only two days later that Traynor was taken down to the baths and afterwards to the ceremony of the Blessed Sacrament. It was here that he felt a tingling sensation in his right arm, and he eventually realised that he could at last move the limb that had been paralysed for the previous eight years. Later that day he could walk seven steps, and he began to feel his reflexes returning. Little by little, Traynor began to feel his limbs returning to normal use, and the following morning he rose from his bed unaided and ran outside for about a half a mile. Shortly after this remarkable occurrence, the pilgrims with whom he had travelled were due to return to Liverpool, but before their departure doctors conducted another examination on Traynor. They were amazed at the extraordinary transformation of his physical condition. Having recovered the use of his lower limbs, he could now walk quite normally, and his right arm had been restored to the condition it had been in prior to the wounds that had been inflicted. Moreover, his epilepsy appeared to have been cured, and doctors also recorded that a hole in his skull that had troubled him for years had all but disappeared. What was equally surprising was the fact that Traynor initially found it very difficult to recall any details of the crippling illness that had beset him for so long. Further examinations were carried out on Traynor on his return to Liverpool, which only confirmed what the medical team at Lourdes already knew. With the evident freedom of movement that he now enjoyed, Traynor was able to work again and, as if to prove once and for all that he had been cured, he set up his own business, occasionally carrying huge sacks of coal with his previously paralysed arm. Because the Government had classed Traynor as 'an incurable and powerless epileptic', he was entitled to a 100 per cent state pension. Evidently, however, Traynor was anything but 'incurable' and 'powerless', and he wrote to the Ministry of Pensions to inform it of his recovery. He was told that he would continue to receive his pension because his 'condition' was such that he would never regain the health that he had once enjoyed.

Traynor continued to make the pilgrimage to Lourdes almost every year until he died in 1943 at the age of sixty.

Delizia Cirollie

The tale of John Traynor has been told countless times since its occurrence in the 1920s. It is interesting to note, however, that the Roman Catholic hierarchy did not proclaim his recovery as being literally miraculous in origin. One such case that the Vatican did consider to be an example of a miracle was the case of Delizia Cirollie. Her experience at Lourdes, and her subsequent cure, is one of the most recent incidents at the shrine to be approved by the Vatican as being the result of heavenly intervention.

Delizia was a twelve-year-old girl who lived in a small village near Mount Etna in Sicily when in 1976 her right knee began causing her severe pain. She was referred to a specialist clinic at the University of Catania, where an X-ray and biopsy revealed a huge protuberance of bone. It was a far worse condition than had been thought. Because Delizia was a minor, the decision rested with her parents as to what the next course of action should be, and they refused to heed the advice of the medical team, who informed them that amputation would be the most humane method of combating such a crippling disease.

Delizia's parents were able to afford a visit to Lourdes in August of that year as a result of the sympathy and generosity of her family, friends and neighbours, although initially it seemed that the pilgrimage would have no beneficial effect whatsoever, with no signs of any miraculous healing process on her afflicted knee, despite the daily rituals that she so faithfully performed. In fact, the growth on her knee began to protrude even more, and, despite the continued prayers for her recovery and her daily intake of water from the spring, most people, including Delizia herself, were sadly accepting that the young girl had very little time left to live.

Then, in December of that year, the miracle happened. She was able to walk again, albeit a short distance at first, but soon she was able to walk for long periods of time without feeling any pain. Her convalescence was finally complete when the protuberance on her knee disappeared. The medical experts at Lourdes held differing views on the precise nature of the growth, and it was not until several years later that it was diagnosed that Delizia had been suffering from a rare form of cancer known as Ewing's tumour – a disease that nobody before Delizia had recovered from.

Divine intervention or rational explanation?

'It is our judgement that Mary, the Immaculate Mother of God, did really appear to Bernadette Soubirous in February 1858 and on certain subsequent days – to the number of eighteen times in all – in the grotto of Massabielle, near the

town of Lourdes; that this Apparition bears
every mark of truth and that the faithful are jus-
tified in believing it as certain.'

(Extract from a report on a special commission
set up by the Bishop of Tarbes)

The Roman Catholic church has often been
criticised for its unflinchingly dogmatic views on
certain subjects. It is only fair to state, however,
that the authorities in the Vatican do not hold a
rigid dogma relating to the many instances of
faith healing at Lourdes. The complex doctrine of
the Immaculate Conception was approved in
Rome in 1854, only four years before the vision
appeared before Bernadette and declared herself
to be the Mother of Jesus. The extraordinary
events in Lourdes could have prompted the Roman Catholic church to declare that a belief in the
doctrine of the Immaculate Conception and a belief that the visions that Bernadette beheld were
the Virgin Mary were inextricably linked, but the
Church has never stated that the apparitions constitute an article of faith, although some would
simply regard this standpoint as an example of the
inherent conservatism of the Catholic hierarchy. It

must not be assumed, therefore, that the church
has a fixed attitude regarding alleged miracle cures
at the shrine. We need only remind ourselves of
the tiny minority of cures that the Church has officially proclaimed as miraculous to realise that this
is not the case. The criteria for deciding whether a
miracle could have brought about a restoration of
health to a person previously afflicted was issued
by Pope Benedict XIV in the eighteenth century.
Seven conditions had to be met:

1 The disability or disease must be exceedingly
   difficult or even impossible to cure, as well as
   being an illness of a very serious nature.
2 The possibility of the invalid making a recovery
   from such an illness must be nonexistent.
3 If the person had received previous medical
   treatment, this treatment must be proved to
   have had no beneficial effect.
4 The cure must occur almost at once.
5 The cure must be complete.
6 It must be proved that the cure did not arise
   from natural causes.
7 There must be no relapse of the illness from
   which the invalid has recovered.

These guidelines are strictly applied, and as a direct result many alleged cases of miracle cures are rejected as non-miraculous. The panel of doctors who study the cases are chosen for their objectivity. The argument for cures arising directly as a result of divine intervention seems strong, but this has not prevented the cynics from attempting to debunk many purported cures.

One of the most notable sceptics was Dr D. J. West, a former President of the Society for Psychical Research, a man thought to have an open mind on matters relating to psychic phenomena. He found much of the evidence for cures self-contradictory. His report, *Eleven Lourdes Miracles*, was published in 1957 after visiting Lourdes and painstakingly examining the medical records relating to miracle cures. Dr West found that the details of many cases were not as scrupulously kept as had previously been thought. He began to doubt that the original diagnosis of the doctors of particular illnesses were 100 per cent accurate.

He also found that in some cases the doctors could not offer conclusive proof that the patients had not already started to recover before they made the pilgrimage to Lourdes. Furthermore, he found that no proof could be offered that the patients whose cases he examined were suffering from incurable illnesses or disease.

Also, in several of the cases that he chose to study, there were disagreements between members of the medical team, who were unable to decide whether or not the cures defied scientific or medical explanation.

In fairness to Dr West, his report did not actually state that miraculous events did not actually take place at Lourdes, only that the evidence that appeared to lend credibility to the miraculous eradication of illnesses was not as conclusive as it was originally thought to be.

Dr West's report came in for severe criticism from Professor David Morrell, who worked at St Thomas's Hospital in London. He stated correctly that of the eleven cases studied by Dr West, none had proved to have been recoveries that came about as a result of natural causes. Professor Morrell pointed out that *Eleven Lourdes Miracles* concentrated on cases from the 1930s and 1940s, when medical tests were much more reliant on clinical findings for the diagnosis of illness. Moreover, he argued that there could obviously be no way of knowing whether an invalid would be miraculously cured following a visit to Lourdes. If it had been known, then previous medical records would undoubtedly have been more carefully kept, he argued. Professor Morrell was particularly condemnatory of Dr West's assertion that hysteria, neurosis and suggestibility were present in some of the cases that he studied. As Professor Morrell said:

'If I see a paralysed patient with contraction flex or spasms and gross neurological signs suddenly cured, I find this difficult to explain irrespective of the diagnosis. The startling thing to me about these cases is that desperately ill patients got suddenly better and stayed better. This is hardly typical of hysterical or functional illness . . . .'

We must not overlook the fact that the great majority of visitors to Lourdes are not people suffering from incurable illnesses, but tourists who arrive there simply to satisfy their curiosity and generally enjoy their holiday. This is worth mentioning because it is easy for the sick to get carried away by the sheer atmosphere that Lourdes engenders, which could leave some of them open to suggestibility. This was doubtless the case when Princess Grace of Monaco arrived at Lourdes with a pilgrimage from her country. One of the pilgrims claimed that a wound on her leg had suddenly disappeared, and many were quick to proclaim this as a miracle. It soon became clear, however, that the wound, which was sustained in a serious road accident, would have disappeared anyway. It was merely a coincidence that the wound began to heal when she visited Lourdes. Of course, stories like this do nothing to explain the mystery of miracle cures, which are presently beyond the realms of scientific explanation.

Many believers in the healing powers of Lourdes often claim that the doctors of some patients have refused to cooperate and have been reluctant to take part in the investigative process. This is cited as one of the reasons why, in some cases, subsequent examinations have not resulted in the cures being called miraculous. This is not as fanciful as it may sound at first. Nowadays the medical profession has a more open-minded approach to the Lourdes phenomenon, but it was not always so. Such was the degree of scepticism with

which the profession viewed events at Lourdes
that a doctor who was brave enough to put forward the view that a miracle may have occurred
risked being laughed out of his job. Little wonder
that so few doctors were willing to cooperate.

This hostility is perhaps best typified by the
story of Alexis Carrell in 1902. A young French
doctor, who was awarded the Nobel Prize for
medicine in 1912, Carrell went on a pilgrimage to
Lourdes, more out of curiosity than anything else.
He became aware that one of the sick pilgrims
was in such a bad condition that she was spitting
blood. Her pulse rate was alarmingly high and her
face had turned blue. Carrell concluded that she
was suffering from tuberculosis. He was amazed
to observe that once the girl had felt the bath
water and taken part in the blessed sacrament pro-
cession, she was cured of her illness. In Carrell's
book, *Journey to Lourdes*, he defied the scepticism of his profession by stating that many events
at Lourdes 'prove the reality of certain links
between psychological and organic processes.
They prove the objective value of spiritual
activity which have been ignored by doctors,
teachers and sociologists.'

It was opinions such as these that only increased the hostility of his colleagues at the university in Lyons where he lectured, and he was forced to leave. What aggrieved Carrell was the fact that his colleagues were so willing to dismiss events he had seen take place in front of his own eyes.

To conclude, we are forced to admit that we are not much nearer to unravelling the mystery of Lourdes than we were when the apparitions first appeared to Bernadette in 1858. Tests have shown that the water at the spring at Lourdes is no more remarkable than the water that we use in everyday life. What is remarkable, of course, is that many people have made recoveries after having come into contact with the water. Until such time as advances in science and medicine can settle these arguments, however, the mystery of Lourdes will remain unsolved.

In this book we would hope to avoid slobbering over the slippers of faith healing and present the subject fairly. This entails telling a few truths about the nature of disease. Anyone who would advocate the use of faith healing or a visit to a shrine should consider the following points carefully:

The variability of disease

With every disease that has a fatal outcome, there are some patients who fare better than the average. For example, in one study, 2 per cent of patients with widespread liver metastases from colorectal cancer survived for five years. These survivors could not ascribe their good fortune to effective treatment, for none was available to them. Instead they demonstrate the natural variability of disease.

In many diseases, such as cancer and multiple sclerosis, a patient's progress follows an oscillating route but a route that is generally moving downwards. Many patients will find that their condition suddenly alleviates and plateaus for a time, even although the general trend is downwards. Many doctors and healers in contact with the sufferer will take the credit for this apparent return to health, playing on the ignorance of the sufferer. Yet it is a rudimentary of logic that because C follows B, we cannot therefore say that B caused C. B here, of course, is the visit to the healer or conventional doctor and C the remission of the illness. All that has happened is a plateauing stage in a downward spiral. The later deterioration to a condition worse than before is frequently out of the public eye and conveniently disregarded.

The respected American cancer researcher Emil J Freireich codified this phenomenon into the 'Freireich Experimental Plan', which demonstrated that any treatment administered to an illness could be proved to have been effective.

Neurotic patients can often experience rapid fluctuations in the progress of their illness. Unexpected improvements can and do occur over a given length of time, and it is such an event that problematises the work of the healer. This phenomenon is usually known as 'spontaneous remission'. Clearly, a cold will eventually go away no matter what you do, even if you do nothing at all.

Most visitors to a faith healer will be at their lowest ebb. For them the only way is up – and although not to deny the therapeutic value of the healer, it is likely that in cases where patients enjoyed a sudden improvement, they were on an upward surge that would have happened anyway.

Faith healers also have the dice loaded in their favour because the majority of people who will

come to them for treatment will be fairly well
educated when it comes to medicine, at least educated enough to be aware of the possibilities of
healing and complementary therapy. What occurs
is a form of medicinal natural selection; extremely disturbed patients, such as sexual devi-
ants and alcoholics, will probably be unaware of
the potential of complementary therapy or not regard it as a possible line of enquiry.

Another problem is that the healer has a vested
interest in declaring his or her treatment a success
and may assess events accordingly. The patients
of faith healers themselves are scarcely any more
objective. The typical account of a healing will
run something like this:

I believe with all my heart that in February
19— I witnessed a healing, a healing that cannot be adequately explained by the normal dictates of medicine. My daughter Sally has been
rescued from the jaws of death, and I wish to
proclaim God's work through your journal.

My daughter was born with a closed pylorus,
the sphincter that connects the stomach with the
bowel. Consequently Sally could not retain

even a thimbleful of milk or a Farley's rusk, and without such nourishment, the child grew alarmingly weak, and her body grew smaller and smaller until everyone concluded that she was on the verge of death.

We first sent for a priest, who bent down and kneeled at the foot of the bed. We earnestly hoped for some upturn, and watched her day and night. Yet it seemed our prayers were not answered and we began to fear the worst.

One evening, during this critical period, a friend of the family happened to mention that she was friendly with a member of the local Christian Science network. Having been ushered into the house in an atmosphere of hope and trepidation, the practitioner confidently went to work. By morning Sally was able to take a full glass of milk and retain it. We thank the Lord for saving our daughter, and we are now firm Christian Scientists.

A passage like this inevitably plays to our emotions, indeed, it is an appeal to our emotionalism. It would be a hard heart indeed that queried the truth of it. There is probably something very deep within human beings that wants to believe in stories like this and that healers can make a difference to the sorry lot of ordinary men and women who are unfortunate enough to be plagued by illness. The truth is that humankind, to all intents and purposes, is powerless against the onslaught of disease. This is a truth that few of us would not find hard to stomach.

Disease is still mysterious to us. One day, a cell becomes cancerous. It begins to eat away at the other cells that surround it, forming a colony. This colony is detected and then destroyed, but colonies of the same cancer begin to appear elsewhere. Still no one can adequately explain why this happens.

Another prime example of the enigma of illness is disseminated sclerosis, a disease in which degeneration occurs in the myelin sheath of the nerve fibres of the brain and spinal cord. The cause of the disease is unknown, and there is no known cure. Death usually results from pneumonia or chronic urinary infection. The tendency to spontaneous improvement is a remarkable feature of the early stages of the disease and can make diagnosis and acceptance of diagnosis and sup-

posed cure problematic for all concerned. The
function of the doctor is to administer the pallia-
tive use of drugs, the inverse of the homeopathic
art of healing.

Healing and hysteria

A highly charged religious atmosphere surrounding the place of pilgrimage, such as Lourdes, or a
healing session can sometimes influence a patient
and imbue him or her with a desire to combat the
illness that once they had regarded as a fait
accompli. Urged on by the atmosphere of excite-
ment and by dramatic renderings from the plat-
form, cripples elatedly throw away their crutches
and the once blind claim their sight has been miraculously restored. There is known to be a form
of hysteria observable at mass healing gatherings
in which the illness of the patient is temporarily
cast aside, and he or she can confidently walk up
and down the stage and appear to have been
healed. Such phenomena are usually ephemeral
and the patients return to their former state once
the show is over. An instance of this occurred
when the American faith healer Maurice Cerullo
visited Britain in 1992. He staged a mass healing

during which a young girl, called Natalia Barned, who was confined to a wheelchair was seen to walk across his stage unaided. What had happened was probably a triumph of will on the part of the young girl. What is key here is the emotional state of the sufferer – it is known that during periods of religious ecstasy the symptoms of quite serious illnesses can be temporarily alleviated.

These factors – the variability of illness, the short-termism of many healing cures and our own emotionalism, considered together – should all be kept in mind when assessing the validity of healing. But we should also bear in mind that none of this necessarily negates the practice of healing, as cures do occur that cannot be refuted by these factors.

Chapter 4

Christian Science

Socially, politically and economically, early nineteenth-century America was experiencing a great deal of changes. This was soon to be intensified by the Civil War (1861–65). The mood of stern Calvinism was gradually changing, and new quasi-scientific movements began to appear. New England and New York had become hotbeds of interest in all things connected with unconventional medicine. The nineteenth century can fairly be described as the golden age of the quack doctor. Mass education had brought with it the popular press with a large uncritical readership ready to swallow any miracle as long as it was framed in pseudo-scientific language. Doctors were thin on the ground and Science had caught the popular imagination and added a new irresistible frisson to the ancient practice of quackery, which had previously had to rely on folklore and superstition for its credibility.

The 1890s saw the rise to prominence of Mary Morse Baker, better known as Mary Baker Eddy (1821–1910). Mark Twain called her 'the most daring and masculine woman that has appeared on the earth in centuries'. It was this New Hampshire mystagogue who founded the Christian Science movement.

Formative years

Mary's upbringing was pervaded by a claustrophobic Calvinism provided by her father, Mark Baker. Her mother's death in childbirth in 1849, when Mary was a teenager, profoundly affected her. It would be the first of many deaths of people that were close to her in her life. Throughout her childhood she was given to temper tantrums, usually brought about by arguments with her father. These tantrums graduated to hysteria and even visions in her adolescent years. Once she claimed to hear voices calling her 'three times in ascending scale', a story that echoes the Biblical story of

Samuel. She was also given to extended bouts of dieting, which would bring her to an almost emaciated state. When the traumas of adolescence became too much she could be restored to equanimity only by being rocked like a child in the arms of her father, a fact that more than one psychologist has seized on in search of the illuminating principle of her life.

At twenty-two she married George Washington Glover, a building contractor eleven years her senior. His death from yellow fever the following year, 1844, left Baker with a son, her only child, and financially virtually penniless. Her child was eventually fostered, and they would enjoy an ambivalent relationship for the rest of their lives.

Phineas Parkhurst Quimby

Mary's next husband, a dentist by the name of Patterson, eventually left her, but by this point she had met the figure who would dictate the future course of her life, Phineas Parkhurst Quimby (1802–66). Baker, on hearing of the miraculous cures being administered by Quimby, decided to travel to Maine from Boston in order to gain an audience with this Swedenborgian. She and

Quimby first met at the International Hotel in
Portland, Maine, in October 1862. Baker was immediately taken by his ideas and his personal
magnetism. He was a healer who denied the efficacy of medicine and proposed instead that the
only real curative force was that of the patient's
belief in the healer and his ability to heal. Quimby
possessed a strong personal magnetism, and although he was poorly educated he managed to
mould his experiences into a philosophy; he
founded the anti-materialist Swedenborgian
school of New Thought, whose following included at least a dozen other American healers.
Quimby claimed disarmingly that his cures were
not due to any paranormal force but instead
merely to the faith that his various patients had in
him, and this alone. Quimby opined: 'I tell the patient his troubles, and what he thinks is his disease, and my explanation is the cure.'

His results were obtained by placing his hand on
the patient's head and abdomen in order to let the
healing magnetic forces take hold. In this he believed that he had rediscovered the very method
that Jesus had employed in healing. He would
eventually discard his mesmerism for a meta-

physical form of faith healing. Quimby was significant in the history of faith healing because he forged a link between the use of the hypnotic and the wholly suggestive approaches, as he progressed from the former to the latter in his career.

Quimby urged that we 'think good, not evil'. If the mind could be cleared of negative thoughts, then this would lead to a healthy body. Baker told Quimby that she had been suffering from 'spinal inflammation'. The cure administered by Quimby began to be effective even before their consultation – her anticipation built up to such an extent that she felt better even before he ministered to her. His treatment ensured that she could walk normally and climb stairs again. Eventually she succumbed to invalidity and gastric pains once more, but she had become a firm believer in Quimby's ideas, although prior to meeting Quimby she had written 'If I believe I am sick, I am sick . . . all disease is in the mind.' She spent the next two years adapting Quimby's philosophy to her own ideas and would one day dismiss him as an 'illiterate mesmerist' and deride his mesmerism as a 'big bubble', an idea she had long been disabused of.

In October 1865, Eddy's father died. Quimby himself met with illness. He had resisted orthodox medicine in the treatment of his illness, a stomach ulcer, and instead insisted that his illness could be brought to heel by the power of his own 'active will'. He died in January 1866.

In February 1866 came the formative moment, when Baker slipped on a icy patch in the street and was knocked unconscious. She claimed her miraculous recovery was accountable to her reliance on the Bible. From being an incurable invalid, she recovered enough to be able to walk around unaided. Some commentators have speculated that Baker's illness was the result of a neurotic depressive reaction. As the Christian Science movement grew her health continued to fluctuate wildly, depending on her mood and situation.

This single-minded child of the Calvinist gloom appropriated a mixture of the ideas of Quimby and German metaphysics in the development of her movement. Some observers describe Christian Science as an amalgam of a metaphysical system that relies on an obsolete theory of logical monism adjusted from the German Idealists, a Christian sect and a method of therapy.

Publication of *Science and Health*

Her ideas (Quimby had already used the term
'Christian Science' in describing his philosophy)
were formally enunciated in her magnum opus,
Science and Health. Her hypothesis was that 'the
only realities are the divine mind and its
ideas . . . . Rightly understood, instead of possess-
ing sentient matter, we have sensationless bodies . . . . Whence came to me this conviction in
antagonism to the testimony of the human senses?
From the self-evident fact that matter has no sensation; from the common human experience of
the falsity of all material things; from the obvious
fact that mortal mind is what suffers, feels, sees:
since matter cannot suffer.'

Baker also wrote: 'I cannot be supermodest in
my estimation of the Christian Science textbook'.
This perhaps unconsciously ironic appraisal of
the bible of the Christian Science movement
comes from the *Christian Science Journal* of
1901. In writing the book she had 'borrowed' ver-
batim thirty-three pages of a work by the scholar
Francis Lieber, which dealt with the work of the
German philosopher Hegel. Another hundred
pages of Lieber's work she simply reworded. This

reworking of ideas already extant was, in truth, completely appropriate to the spirit of all the other competing forms of Christian healing at the time, which were all variations on a theme compounded of contemporary religious ideas, occult practices and metaphysics, with the leaders of these various sects all drawing from the same well.

Other aspects of the movement were probably appropriated from other sects; for example, her advocacy of silent prayer was taken from Quakerism. It is ironic that one of her former students, called Arens, was sued by her for infringing her copyright on Christian Science ideas in his book *Old Theology in its Application to the Healing of the Sick*. She was renowned for the swift repression of any potential rivalry for the leadership of the movement.

In 1877 she married for a third time, aged fifty-six, to a forty-five-year-old agent for a sewing machine manufacturer, called Asa Gilbert Eddy. Like her, he also suffered from poor health. A passive recipient of his wife's doctrines, he was the first acolyte to become a public convert to the Church of Christ, Scientist, which she founded in Boston in 1879. Although supposedly cured of assorted abdominal and chest pains by his wife, Asa's pains returned after a short interval. Like Quimby before him, he insisted that he could control the pains himself. Eddy claimed that her husband was being 'mentally murdered' by means of animal magnetism employed by her enemies. This streak of paranoia became marked in her later years. For instance, she ascribed her public maligning and ridicule, as well as her personal misfortune, to the result of an unseen baleful influence, what she called 'animal magnetism'. Eventually they resorted to orthodox medicine for treatment. Organic heart disease was diagnosed and later confirmed at Asa's autopsy. Eddy refused to accept this diagnosis and insisted that an unseen psychic Mafia had murdered her husband.

Eddy's wealth

Mary Baker Eddy eventually left Boston and retired to Concord, visiting the centre of Christian Science in Boston only another four times in her life, although still maintaining a strong grip on the movement and its organisation to the end of her life. She founded a college and a newspaper and lectured continuously until she died of pneumonia in 1910. Like Mesmer, she managed to accumulate a fortune from her religious healing work. Membership of the Christian Science movement rose to a peak in the 1930s with an estimated 300,000 members. Since then membership has drastically fallen as Christian Science has had to compete in the marketplace with other sects.

Although the name of Christ appears in the movement's title, Eddy did write: 'If there had never existed such a Galilean prophet (Jesus) it would make no difference to me.' (*Science and Health*). This denial of the role of the physician goes against the use of the physician advocated in the Bible, specifically in Ecclesiastes:

'The Lord hath created medicines out of the earth; and he that is wise will not abhor them . . . . Give place to the physician, for the Lord hath created him; let him not go from thee, for thou hast need of him. There is a time when in their hands there is good success.'

It is difficult to assess the Christian Science movement. There is little attention to charity, no interest in any supernatural power, and health and wealth are promised to its followers, who are and were mainly middle class. Christian Science could happily deny the reality of matter but did not so easily deny the value of money. At the end of her life, Eddy had become a wealthy woman, with a fortune estimated at upwards of four million dollars. To take a short course at her 'metaphysical college' cost 300 dollars alone.

The Christian Science movement's views on healing can appear to be inconsistent. Some members will employ the use of dentists, doctors, opticians and doctors, if need be. Indeed, Eddy herself used drugs, especially morphine to dull pain, on numerous occasions towards the end of her life. Beyond this, there are ethical problems with the philosophy of the group. Treating all pain as delusional instead of as a warning sign that demands enquiry into the cause is obviously foolish, as is risking the aggravation of a depression in a patient, brought about by telling him or her that his or her illness is both delusional and equivalent to sin and, by extension, the fault of the patient. For instance, Eddy denied that food promulgated life – she was given to making remarks such as 'we have no evidence of food sustaining life, except false evidence'.

Eddy's teaching on the unreality of matter, sin and suffering seems to conflict with the Biblical doctrines of the Creation, Fall and Redemption. It should also be remembered that Jesus himself made no comment that could reasonably be interpreted as hostile to the physical medicine of his time.

Christian Science also has its own individual slant on healing, although the movement is not primarily curative in aim. The distinction between the Christian Scientist and that of the standard faith healer on the matter of healing is that, while the faith healer holds that pain and disease are actually illusions of the imagination, he or she acknowledges their existence but affirms the possibility of their removal by non-scientific means.

Mary Baker Eddy's personal philosophy could be rather strange. For example, on the health of infants, she advises: 'The condition of the stomach, bowels, food, clothing, etc, is of no serious importance to your child.' The Christian Scientist is happy if his patient knows little or nothing, because 'a patient thoroughly booked in on medical theories has less sense of the divine power, and is more difficult to heal through Mind, than an aboriginal Indian who never bowed the knee to the Baal of civilisation.'

As well as reality and food, the idea that pro- creation was what produced life came in for some heavy criticism: 'Until it is learned that genera- tion rests on no sexual basis, let marriage con- tinue . . . . The suggestion that life germinates in eggs is shown by divine metaphysics to be a mis- take' (quoted in Godwin).

Some passages of *Christian Science* are just plained confused: 'The nothingness of nothing is plain; but we need to understand that error is noth- ing, and that its nothingness is not saved, but must be demonstrated in order to prove the somethingness . . . of Truth.'

She claimed to have administered one cure by preaching to a horse. Perhaps it should be said that to mock the ideas of Christian Science is tak- ing an easy target. We should remember that Ed- dy's time was not our own before we rush to judge her approach to healing. It would be the turn of the century before Sigmund Freud and Carl Jung stated that certain illnesses could reside in the un- conscious mind.

Eddy's philosophies

'In less than three weeks from the time of us
turning to Christian Science treatment,
Kristen's burn was completely covered with
fresh skin. There was no need for a bandage any
more, and the visible signs of the burn were
fading. Kristen was back in her Kindergarten
class shortly thereafter. Christian Science treatment was continued and she now walks and
runs normally . . . .'

So speaks another happy customer of the Christian Science approach. Yet Kristen's burn would
no doubt have healed substantially after the space
of three weeks given no treatment whatsoever. As
Disraeli once said, 'Time is the great physician'.
Note we are told that this 'three weeks' is only the
three weeks since the Christian Science treatment
began, not since the burn was incurred. One has to
ask precisely what would constitute failure for
Christian Science treatment in the light of this.
We should bear in mind that 80 to 90 per cent of
illnesses recover under any treatment or with absolutely no treatment.

    Medical training and registration were still in a

rudimentary state in Eddy's time, so her self-awarded title of 'doctor' would have been honorary. In England the Apothecaries Act of 1815 stopped unqualified doctors from practising medicine. Yet we cannot deny this able commander her due, which resided in her tremendous organisational ability. Her youthful girlish appearance was a great asset, presenting both a physically attractive woman with dark brooding eyes but at the same time a 'safe' mother figure, which appealed to the many insecure and neurotic males who attended her. Other competing contemporary religious movements, such as Andrew Jackson Davis's doctrines of life health and cures, failed to show the staying power of Eddy's movement, even though during the 1840s his movement was as big as Christian Science in terms of popularity. Jackson simply did not have the drive and ambition and sheer blind energy of Eddy. In her favour, Mrs Eddy's positive encouraging nature must have consoled the many who felt forsaken by conventional medicine.

As was once said of Oscar Wilde, Eddy stood in direct symbolic relation to her time. Virtually all her adult life was spent during the reign of Queen

Victoria, which also coincided with the emergence of the emancipation for women movement and the fight for female suffrage. Mrs Eddy and her followers were a great boost to the female cause as it was highly unusual at the time for a woman to be giving lectures and addressing public meetings.

Another means by which she captured the zeitgeist was by grasping, either consciously or unconsciously, the need for a movement that would alleviate religious insecurities by reconciling the old Christian orthodoxy with the unknown element of the new emergent science – although, of course, there was very little or nothing about the movement that could be called truly scientific – nevertheless, she intimately understood what was needed to massage and reassure the psychological hurts and uncertainties that lay deep in the American psyche. She anticipated the mood of the middle classes and catered to it. Christian Science's advocacy of 'healthy-mindedness', as William James put it, coupled with an open and receptive attitude to materialism, told the middle classes exactly what they wanted to hear. Mrs Eddy's receptivity to her public was truly awe-inspiring. No doubt she would have made an excellent politician in another time. She also anticipated many of the practices of modern medicine. The modern psychological approach to chronic pain is based on the relief of anxiety, distraction and suggestion, which is strikingly similar to the approach advocated by Eddy. In a sense, Eddy's hypothesis is correct – unhappiness and suffering do indeed only exist in the mind; it is her contention that illness and disease do not have objective existence that one has to refute.

In the various photographs taken of Eddy we see a wistful melancholic face – a face remarkably similar to that of Greatrakes – with black hair framing eyes brimming with soulful intensity. In the two most commonly printed photographs of her she appears to be quietly amused at some inward joke to herself. Perhaps the joke was on us.

Chapter 5

Spiritual Healing Therapies

Outside the realm of the evangelist and the healing ministries of the church, there is a whole different movement that embraces the healing ethic while not wishing to limit itself to the confines of a particular religious doctrine. The spiritual healer seeks to provide for the large sections of society that do not subscribe to any given religious system but do acknowledge the spiritual dimension of their existence.

In addition, spiritual healers reject the term 'faith healing' because, apart from suggesting a required religious belief, it implies that the patient must at least have faith in the healer's capacity to heal in order for the treatment to have any effect.

This has been proved not to be the case, as on their list of successful healings, spiritual healers can include children, animals and even plants, which are presumably incapable of faith. Even the most hardened sceptic can be healed; the only thing that the patient is required to believe in is that he or she wants to be well.

Nowadays, the term 'spiritual healing' specifically refers to the type of healing practised by the National Federation of Spiritual Healers (NFSH), which has around 8,000 healers on its register. Spiritual healing is, in fact, listed as a recognised therapy within the National Health Service; GPs are permitted by the General Medical Council to refer their patients for spiritual healing, and it is possible for NFSH healers to visit hospital inpatients on request. Some enlightened doctors do actually realise that good health is more than simply an absence of illness, and that a state of spiritual imbalance can be as debilitating as a physical disorder.

Spiritual healers address themselves to the nonphysical aspect of being, working on the level of the spirit or soul rather than that of the body. They direct healing energy to the inner essence of an individual, and if this vital spark responds, the body's healing mechanisms can be activated.

The other definitively 'spiritual' element of spiritual healing is the source of its healing power. Where the faith healer invokes the will of God to heal, the spiritual healer calls upon the power of nature, or the all-pervasive life force that unites us.

It should be pointed out at this stage that spiritual healing is not to be confused with spiritualist healing. Spiritualism entails a fervent belief in the after-life as its basis and effects its healing through communication with dead spirits. This form of healing is discussed later, in Chapter 8, Healing and the Occult.

There are two basic types of spiritual healing – contact and absent.

Contact healing is the more common form employed by healers, usually identified by the term 'the laying on of hands'. This phrase has distinctly mystical, and even biblical, connotations, but in fact it is a very simple procedure, performed in order to implement healing. It is perhaps the oldest, and certainly the simplest, type of healing in existence. Everyone knows the therapeutic value of the intimacy of touch. When a fellow human being is in distress we instinctively reach out a hand to place on his or her arm or shoulder, and this gesture is immediately recognised to be both comforting and reassuring.

Obviously, the laying on of hands by professional healers goes beyond simply making someone 'feel better'. It is their way of transferring vital energy to the patient, thus stimulating the body's natural restorative mechanisms and enabling the healing process to be set into motion.

The 'laying on of hands' denotes exactly that – the healer lays his or her hands either directly on, or just above, the patient's body. The hands are usually placed on the head or shoulders, or on a specifically affected part of the body. Sometimes a healer likes to move his or her hands down the spine, an important part of the human body that can reveal ailments in other regions. Many healers are able to diagnose with their hands, as well as heal, although this is not advisable in place of a proper medical examination and diagnosis. This method does, however, help to guide the healer to the areas of the body where energy levels have become depleted because of illness or injury. The healer will sense an imbalance and be able to restore lost energy by passing life force through the hands. The patient will usually experience a sensation of heat in the area where the problem is located. This is the thermal energy, visible using Kirlian photography, that is transmitted through the touch of the healer's hands and penetrates the body in much the same way as scientifically proven deep heat treatment. The process of replacing lost energy usually feels wonderful for the recipient, inducing a feeling of calmness, contentment and deep relaxation.

This transfer of energy may sound like a form of magic, but no genuine spiritual healer would ever claim to possess special, mystical powers. All honest healers acknowledge that they themselves neither create nor possess healing power or energy but merely act as channels for a higher power. Their talent is not the gift of healing but the gift of being able to tap into universal healing energy.

Most spiritual healers who practise contact healing also practise absent or distant healing. As the name suggests, the healing is performed in the patient's absence, sometimes even without their knowledge. The principles of harnessing the healing forces and channelling them to the patient remain the same, however. In this case the positive energy is transmitted in the form of a healing message. The healer sends out healing vibrations while clearly visualising the recipient in perfect health, perhaps bathed in ethereal light. Sometimes the name of the sufferer is spoken out loud, creating a telepathic link along which the energy can travel. The nature of the illness to be cured, however, should not be uttered or even thought about, because this will add potency to the illness in the mind and make it grow stronger.

Absent healing is obviously particularly suitable for patients living far away, but also for children, animals, the mentally deranged, the chronically ill and those who are unconscious in a coma. Absent healing can be highly beneficial for anyone who is incapable of taking an active part in his or her own healing. It does not matter that the recipient may not be actively receptive to the healing vibrations – as long as he or she is not sending out negative counter-healing messages there will still be benefit.

Radionics is a slightly more dubious form of

distant healing, involving specially designed instruments. A 'black box' is employed that can pick up the electromagnetic radiations emitted by all living things. The instrument can be used as a diagnostic tool by tuning into 'diseased' wavelengths and translating them into electrical frequencies, determining an individual's mental, physical and emotional state. By transmitting vibrationally suitable wavelengths, the unsatisfactory condition can be cured. This all sounds very technical, drawing from the laws of physics, but in fact the practice of radionics is highly unscientific and relies largely on the intuition and sensitivity of the practitioner. There is, in fact, no scientific evidence of the effectiveness of radionics nor any logical reason why it should work.

Now that you know a little about the basic ways in which spiritual healers operate, and the techniques they employ, we should focus on how to find a suitable healer.

Finding the name and address of a spiritual healer in your area is relatively easy, as the NFSH provides lists (*see* Useful Addresses), but finding a healer who works for you, and with whom you feel comfortable, may be a different matter. Basically it is a question of using your intuition and listening to your instincts. Healing is a two-way process, and it is important that a mutual bond is established between healer and patient, allowing the free passage of healing energy from one to the other. The patient must therefore feel fully at ease with the chosen healer and be able to relax and express himself or herself freely in the healer's presence.

Spend a bit of time chatting to the healer before you commit yourself to undergoing a session of treatment. If you feel at all uncomfortable with him or her, do not be afraid to suggest that perhaps he or she is not the right practitioner for you and leave. Do not accept treatment from a healer who appears tired or weak; he or she obviously does not know how to harness the healing life force properly and may even drain you of whatever vital energy you have. Also, be on the lookout for anything that seems vaguely self-serving in the healer's character, behaviour or manner, such as traces of ego or lust. The role of the healer as lover is discussed in Chapter 9, Roles of the Healer, but in this situation, dishonourable intentions on either side could become a serious obstacle to effective healing. Genuine healers offer their services out of a sincere wish to use what powers they have to help people in suffering, not for the rewards, either emotional or material, that this may bring.

While on this subject, the question of whether spiritual healers should charge for their services remains a contentious issue. There are those who believe that it is wrong to make money out of desperate, suffering people, but anyone wishing to concentrate on exercising their healing abilities on a full-time basis obviously requires some kind of income. Most healers compromise by asking for donations, and those who charge a fee can usually be negotiated with if there is a real need.

To give you some idea of the different kinds of healing experience that are possible, here are four people's personal stories of spiritual healing. Each illustrates something different that can be achieved through healing while expressing something universal about the nature of the human condition and the healing phenomenon.

Case Study 1

Mick Allstrap, a thirty-two-year-old journalist currently working in Amsterdam, visited a spiritual healer for the first time during a recent return visit to the UK. A card-carrying sceptic, Mick decided to undergo this experience, partly out of journalistic curiosity and partly out of sheer desperation after a string of doctors had been unable to help him.

Mick has suffered from recurrent back problems ever since his teens, when he was the victim of an unprovoked street attack by a gang of youths. The muscle tissues surrounding the vertebrae were damaged, resulting in frequent bouts of intense pain and slightly restricted movement.

The back and spine are complex and vulnerable areas of the body, notoriously difficult to treat effectively. There are a limited number of medical treatments available for a doctor to administer, the most commonly prescribed being painkillers and anti-inflammatory agents, which merely alleviate the discomfort temporarily.

Dissatisfied with the little that orthodox medicine had to offer, Mick decided to bite the bullet and look elsewhere. Through a friend he found the name and address of a Romanian spiritual healer living just outside Glasgow and arranged a session.

Arriving for his appointment full of trepidation,

Mick was pleasantly surprised to be ushered into a brightly lit flat by an elegant middle-aged woman who did not conform to his mental image of a kaftan-wearing New Age casualty.

The woman carried out an immediate psychic appraisal, correctly identifying Mick's back as the 'sick' part of his body, as well as several minor ailments of which he had not been aware. Mick told the healer about the way in which he had sustained the original back injuries, and she nodded sagely.

After taking off his shoes, Mick was asked to lie on his stomach on the treatment bench and to relax and breath deeply. The woman then clasped his feet, one in each hand. Mick could actually feel a flow of energy running from her left hand into his left foot, up his left side and back down his right side, through his right foot into the woman's right hand. He felt the energy forming a complete circuit around his body, which felt wonderful, relaxing and revitalising.

Then the woman focused her energy upon Mick's back, laying her hands on the affected area. It felt as if all the energy that had been circulating his body was suddenly drawn to an epicentre, creating a tremendous amount of heat where the healer's hands were placed. As well as heat, Mick began to experience a substantial amount of pain, even though the woman was not applying any pressure with her hands. She explained that, because of the traumatic way in which his back had come to be in its present state, he had been withholding the pain of the original assault. In order to heal, Mick had to confront the pain, re-experience it and release it.

Before the pain escalated to an unbearable level, the healer ran her hands swiftly down from his back to his feet. This action was accompanied by what Mick could only describe as a 'whooshing' sensation, as the heat and pain travelled down his body and out through the soles of his feet.

On standing up, Mick was delighted to find that the pains in his back had indeed gone, along with a headache he had had that morning. In fact, he felt like a new man. The healer advised him to take life slowly over the following few days as he would probably feel slightly sick and groggy because of the stale energy that had been displaced during the healing gradually eliminating itself from his system.

Several weeks on, and still feeling the benefits,

Mick had to admit that the treatment had worked for him and that something remarkable and inexplicable had taken place. He still, however, remains sceptical as to the source of his healing.

Case Study 2

This next story concerns a young man in his mid-twenties, whom we shall call Declan. Born and brought up in the Stockport area, the only son of an elderly Catholic couple, Declan began to develop obsessive-compulsive disorder, or OCD, at the age of eighteen.

For anyone unfamiliar with this condition, it is a severely debilitating form of mental illness that can have devastating effects on the sufferer's daily life. The disorder usually begins as a phobia, an irrational fear that escalates into an all-consuming obsession. Sufferers often believe that some terrible fate will befall them if they do not carry out particular actions. These actions are often ritualised and performed in a specific pattern, making even the simplest of tasks tortuous.

In Declan's case, his obsessive-compulsive behaviour first manifested itself in a morbid fear of coming into contact with bacteria and germs. This began in church when, during mass, he would be expected to shake hands with the people next to him. The thought of this, and the exchange of bacteria involved, repulsed him in the extreme until he could eventually no longer participate. He also began to dread handling money and having to touch the hands of shop assistants as they handed him change. He could not prevent his mind from dwelling on the idea that some coins could have been in circulation for as long as twenty years, accumulating bacteria that he could not avoid touching.

The next stage was compulsive hand-washing, a common behavioural pattern in OCD sufferers. Declan would perform numerous hand-washing rituals, both before and after completing any given task. Especially before eating or preparing food, he would wash his hands for at least half an hour, scrubbing them with a nail brush.

Declan's parents began to notice that his hands were often red raw until eventually his father confronted him and persuaded him to see a doctor. The doctor referred Declan to a psychiatrist in the hope of uncovering some psychological trigger for this obsessive-compulsive behaviour. The psychiatrist proffered several theories for Declan's condition, centring on some possibly forgotten trauma in infancy combined with Catholic guilt and repression. This diagnosis left Declan more confused and anxious than ever, his head spinning with psycho-babble.

His mother then suggested that he talk to an acquaintance of hers who carried out spiritual healings. This woman, who combined her healing with a full-time teaching job, immediately put Declan at his ease, encouraging him to express the feelings of fear and revulsion that fuelled his behaviour. Then she stood behind him and held her hands just above his shoulders, not touching so as not to activate his OCD. She told him that she was passing vital energy into him, and encouraged him to shut his eyes and imagine the energy flowing into him as a stream of liquid light. Declan could indeed feel a warm tingling sensation entering him and moving around his body. Then the healer urged him to visualise this energy, which now pervaded his body, as extending beyond his body to form a kind of aura completely surrounding him.

He was to imagine this energy force-field as a

protective shell that would allow other people to pass through to make physical contact but would dissolve germs and bacteria on contact before they could reach his body.

After several healing sessions and regular self-help visualisation exercises, Declan has managed to keep his obsessive-compulsive behaviour under control to an extent. As any OCD sufferer will tell you, it is not a problem that ever really goes away – you just have to learn to control and resist the compulsions that threaten you. Declan believes that he now has the strength to fight his phobias and that it was spiritual healing that helped him to achieve this.

Case Study 3

Christine Booth, a fifty-seven-year-old divorcee, was diagnosed as suffering from breast cancer in 1992. After distressing chemotherapy treatment, it became evident that she would have to undergo surgery in order to remove the cancerous growth.

After much soul-searching Christine decided that surgery was indeed her only hope and went into hospital for a mastectomy. Unfortunately, she had taken the step too late, and the operation proved unsuccessful in removing every trace of cancerous tissue. The cancer continued to spread, and Christine's condition was acknowledged to be terminal.

At this point, having accepted that the doctors could do nothing for her now, Christine embarked on a spiritual journey, hoping to find something to help her come to terms with her situation. A life-long atheist, she now realised how scared she was of death and how much she desperately needed the consolation of a spiritual belief.

A chance encounter with a spiritual healer provided her with what she was seeking and marked the way towards a healing of sorts. Christine met Trevor Foster at a supermarket, where they struck up a conversation and immediately established a special rapport. Trevor, a registered healer, had recently lost his wife to cancer, having supported and treated her through several painful years of illness. Trevor extended his help and support to Christine in her hour of need and she accepted his offer of treatment and spiritual guidance.

Over the course of many weeks Trevor channelled positive spiritual energy into Christine. He also taught her meditation and visualisation techniques, and counselled her through emotional low points. Through these actions, Christine's levels of self-awareness and life-awareness soared, and she began to recognise and express the feelings of anger, pain and resentment that she had bottled up all her life, particularly surrounding the breakdown of her marriage. Consequently, she felt a sense of liberation and a reconcilement with life, which in turn instilled in her a sense of calm and completion. She had reached a state of acceptance, free from inner conflict, and was ready to die, knowing that her spirit would be immortal as part of the universal life force that encompasses humankind.

It was at this point that the cancerous cells in her body ceased to multiply and the tumours started to reduce in size. Christine is in no doubt that this was a direct result of Trevor's care and treatment. She believes that when her body was eased of tension, her immune system was given an enormous boost, and her illness began to go into spontaneous regression.

She is still by no means free of the cancer, but she has already significantly stretched the life expectancy allotted to her by her doctors. She continues to battle against the disease with the power of positive belief as her weapon and Trevor as her standard-bearer.

Case Study 4

Most people will be aware of the therapeutic value of animal companionship, as experiments have shown that petting a dog or a cat can significantly reduce stress levels and lower blood pressure. However, not everyone will have heard of a moose possessed of healing powers.

A Canadian moose hit the headlines in the early 1980s when it played the central role in a remarkable story involving a small diabetic boy. The nine-year-old, who had developed diabetes at the age of five, required twice-daily injections of insulin and a strictly controlled diet in order to regulate his blood sugar level.

The boy's parents encouraged him, however, to lead a normal, active life, as diabetes need not be a constraining condition. On this premise, they decided to take their son and his elder brother on a short camping trip. During a game the boy became separated from his family and became lost in the densely forested woodland.

As darkness fell, hampering search rescue attempts, hopes for the boy's safety faded. Having gone without insulin or food for so many hours it was unlikely that he would survive without slipping into a diabetic coma caused by dangerously low blood sugar.

When daylight returned and searches continued afresh, the boy was discovered safe and well in the company of an adult moose. The moose was unwilling to leave the boy's side, adopting an aggressive stance, and eventually had to be frightened away by gunshots being fired into the air. Paramedics who immediately examined the boy found him to be in perfect health, and a test of his blood showed his sugar level to be constant.

It transpired that the boy, realising he was lost, had panicked and run deeper into the forest, trying to find a way out. Starting to feel faint and unsteady, the first symptoms of low blood sugar, he had stopped and huddled in a small clearing. Shortly afterwards, a large dark creature emerged from between the trees and approached the boy. Frozen with terror, as the moose is a fearsome looking beast, especially to a young child, the boy stayed completely still as the animal lay down beside him, pressing its flank against his body. Something about the creature's benign brown eyes reassured the boy, and he thinks he fell asleep, exhausted with running and distress.

He awoke the next morning, no longer feeling faint, to find the moose still at his side. Soon afterwards, the search party arrived and he was reunited with his family.

To this day doctors are baffled as to how the boy survived without insulin, and how his blood sugar level appeared normal. After the incident, the boy continued to require treatment for his diabetes and still receives daily insulin injections.

Later the moose was identified as a female who had recently lost her calf. The theory was put forward that the boy must have suckled from the still lactating moose, but even this would not have been sufficient to raise his blood sugar level to beyond danger point.

The boy, now a young man, strongly believes that the moose exercised some kind of protective healing power over him. While in its presence, he felt a feeling of warm, deep peace and a lifting of physical and mental discomfort.

It would be easy to dismiss this idea out of hand,

simply because it is ridiculous. Mooses healing? Whatever next – pine cones playing ping pong?

When considered without empirical hysteria, however, it becomes apparent that this parable could be illustrative of the power of love and therapeutic touch. The moose, suffused with maternal instincts following the death of her calf, extended her protective love to what she recognised to be a young animal in danger and distress, for which the boy and his family will be eternally grateful.

Sadly, the moose, affectionately christened 'Harriet' by the Canadian public and dubbed 'The Moosiah' by the Canadian press, died shortly afterwards, perhaps in order to escape the stream of prying tourists and misguided pilgrims.

Many people may find these stories hard to believe, but they are representative of the kind of healings that occur week in, week out. They sound incredible because spiritual healing is incredible. It is true that no scientific basis has been identified for the claims made for healing, but this seems trivial and irrelevant in the light of the hundreds of successfully treated people who stand as testimony to their own healing experiences.

Detractors of spiritual healing will say that these cases can all be explained rationally and attributed to the power of suggestion or auto-suggestion, or to the charismatic influence of the healer. These explanations, however, are no more 'rational' than the idea of spiritual healing, as they too work on the unconscious level of the psyche and are intangible to scientific experimentation.

If, as stated previously, the healer simply acts as a channel for the greater forces of life, in theory anyone can develop healing skills. Meditation and contemplative, self searching thought, combined with a genuine love and compassion for humankind and peppered with a touch of intuitive sensitivity, could be the recipe for a healing disposition. The basic requirement is an ability to learn to be receptive to the messages that the mind sends the body and, in time, acquire the ability to control these messages. Self-healing can be the most fulfilling spiritual healing of all, opening up the self to others and becoming one with the universal healing life force.

Chapter 6

Healing-related Therapies

It will have become apparent that most alternative healing processes involve the harnessing and channelling of energy from the healer to the patient. This energy can be perceived in different ways, whether it is believed to be life force, prana, ch'i, divine force, psychic or electromagnetic energy. Some say they can actually see this energy, while most sense it in an abstract, intangible way.

There are many ways in which we can develop and expand the five senses to which we are limited in order to become sensitive to the energy vibrations that surround us somewhere where physics and mysticism meet. By tuning in to the rhythms of the universe we can learn to co-operate with nature's innate healing capacity

Here we have chosen several interconnected therapies, all of which respond to the vibrations of the life-energy around us. They also all are complementary to, and indeed contain elements of, spiritual and faith healing. Some of the same methods are employed in each of them, but they all harness and channel energy differently.

Aura therapy

Many healers believe that as well as a physical body, we all possess a psychic 'body' that extends beyond our corporal form. This is believed to be a force field of spiritual energy that surrounds all living things and connects individuals through a universal source.

The aura, as this force field is called, is thought to comprise all the radiations from the actions and interactions of cells and chemicals in the body, and so reflects the individual's state of health. If the body is suffering from illness, the radiations from the affected organ will be weak, and subsequently dull patches in the aura are perceived.

The aura can stretch up to several metres from the body, or merely several centimetres, and consists of bands of different coloured light, all the colours of the spectrum as well as black, white and grey. Each person's aura is different in shape, colour and definition, and those who can perceive auras say that they can tell a lot about an individual's character and mood as well as the state of his or her physical, emotional and spiritual health.

Practitioners of aura healing are so sensitive to tuning into auras that the colours and shapes of a patient's aura are actually visible to them, not just sensed. Then they can interpret the order and the intensity of these colours, as each colour signifies different emotions, characteristics and disposition to illness. In a proper interpretation of someone's aura, the positioning of the colours in relation to each other is very important, but here is a basic outline of what each colour may signify:

- *Red* – red is the colour of vitality, passion and energy, and someone with a lot of red in his or her aura will be outgoing, physically vigorous and generous of spirit, although an excess indicates selfishness and materialism. Dark red in the aura may be indicative of anger or malice, whereas light red shows anxiety and tension.
- *Orange* – bright orange denotes a strong, ambi-

tious personality and is also associated with good health and energy. A slightly lighter shade of orange signifies a compassionate, considerate and well-adjusted nature, but too much orange in the aura indicates overambitiousness to the detriment of others

- *Yellow* – yellow in the aura shows mental agility and is apparent when someone is concentrating. As well as intellect, yellow also highlights optimism, and gold-yellow shows spirituality and perception. A murky yellow in the aura may indicate weakness, indecisiveness, frustration or suspicion.

- *Green* – green is a healing colour as it is the colour of nature and rebirth. In the aura it shows a vibrant sociable personality and may mean that the individual has the healing gift. A preponderance of green, on the other hand, signifies a lack of empathy with others.

- *Blue* – blue is a very positive colour, associated with idealism, inspiration and integrity. Dark blue indicates specifically religious inspiration and a deeply spiritual nature while pale blue shows a predisposition to scholarship. A dingy blue, however, means negativity.

- *Indigo* – indigo is also a spiritual colour, denoting strong moral values and the search for a higher truth. A lot of indigo in an aura signifies inner calm, serenity and good-naturedness. If it shows up blotchy or weak, this could indicate moodiness and irritability.
- *Violet* – violet is a devotional colour signifying love and spiritual enlightenment. Not everyone possesses a noticeable amount of violet in his or her aura, but those who do have profound insight and spiritual awareness.
- *White* – white represents perfection, the attainment of the highest possible spiritual enlightenment. It signifies truth and purity.
- *Black* – black in the aura shows an emotionally damaged individual. Black represents negative thoughts, destruction and despair.
- *Grey* – grey in the aura usually signifies illness or depression. In rare cases it can denote an individual devoid of personality.

As stated previously, these colours are present in different combinations in every individual and can appear mixed, layered or patchy, depending upon the ailment. Aura healing is not only a diag-

nostic but a curative therapy. Once the therapist
has defined and interpreted the state of a patient's
aura, and feels that he or she fully understands the
problem, there are a number of ways in which the
patient can be treated.

As with other forms of spiritual healing, the
therapist acts as a channel through which universal spiritual energy can flow. Rather than use energy from their own auras, practitioners harness
this greater energy and 'feed' it into the patient's
aura. This could involve increasing the amount of
colour that has become depleted in a particular
area of the aura, or introducing a complementary
colour that will even out any imbalances in the intensity of another colour.

The role of the patient in his or her own healing
is heavily emphasised in this form of therapy. Patients are encouraged to take an active part in the
healing process through self-awareness and positive thinking. Meditation and visualisation exercises can be used to tune into and strengthen the
aura.

Some auric practitioners believe that everyone
has the ability to sense auras, if not actually see
them. We subconsciously pick up the vibrations

that another person's aura sends out, and this is the basis on which we place our impressions of him or her and gauge his or her personality and mood. If an individual makes you feel uneasy it could be because the aura is vibrating in conflict with your own, creating disharmony.

There are ways in which you can develop your ability to sense, or even see, auras. This means adopting an open mind and attitude, and setting aside any scepticism about the existence of auras. Watch people closely and listen very carefully to what they say, with as much empathy as possible. Notice their movements and mannerisms, and observe how they relate to their environment. It is a question of learning to notice and understand the subliminal messages that people continually send out about themselves and their situation.

Of course, there is no scientific evidence to support the existence of auras, although Kirlian photography shows that the body does emit some kind of electromagnetic energy. It could be said that the way in which auric therapists sense moods, emotions and disorders is through a form of observant intuition, itself as intangible as the idea of the aura.

Colour Therapy

Colour therapy is closely linked to aura healing, and the two are often practised in conjunction. The idea of colour therapy goes back to ancient civilisations, as the Greeks and Egyptians are believed to have chosen the colours of their temple adornments for their beneficial effects on the mind, body and spirit. Colour therapy is also still practised in Tibet and India, where Buddhist monks wear orange robes because of the colour's spiritual properties. It has been proven that people are affected both psychologically and physically by different coloured light. What colour healers do is work with the various principles of certain colours to bring about effective healing.

Recent investigation has shown that there is a close correlation between certain colours and states of mind. Colour can affect people's mood, perception of time and temperature, and their ability to concentrate and function effectively. Some colours can induce anxiety and unease while others create a tranquil, restful state of mind. For example, greens and blues are commonly used in the decoration of hospitals and prisons because they have been found to have a relaxing effect, counteracting aggression and anxiety. Even fast-food restaurants know the significance of colour psychology and make use of the colour red to encourage people to eat quickly and move on. The strength of the colour induces a feeling of urgency and discourages the desire to linger.

Colour therapists go beyond psychology and believe that specific maladies can be treated and cured by adjusting the colour input to the body. As with aura therapy, it is believed that the body absorbs the electromagnetic energy of light and gives out its own aura of energy, which vibrates in a specific pattern. An unhealthy body creates an imbalance in this pattern, and the colour therapist strives to restore the balance through the stimulation of bodily reactions by colour. Colour healing is said to be based on the principle of attraction – the vibrations of the colour attract similar vibrations in the human body and extract the vibrations that are causing imbalance and illness.

The main colours used in colour therapy are red, orange, yellow, green, turquoise, blue, violet and magenta. Each colour is considered to be effective in the treatment of specific ailments.

- *Red* – red can be helpful in the treatment of circulatory problems, low blood pressure and anaemia.
- *Orange* – orange is effective on complaints involving the chest and the digestive system.
- *Yellow* – yellow can be used to help sufferers of skin complaints and nervous conditions.
- *Green* – green can treat stress, headaches and emotional disturbances.
- *Blue* – blue also calms the mind and can be used to help ease fevers and complaints of the nervous system.
- *Violet* – violet is helpful in the treatment of rheumatism, epilepsy and nervous disorders.

When making a diagnosis, a colour therapist will ask about your colour preferences as well as for details of your medical history and lifestyle. Most therapists will also employ an element of intuition or extrasensory perception to assess any imbalances in your aura.

Then the therapist will concentrate on your spine, stroking the length of it while focusing on your condition. Each vertebra relates to a part of the body as well as to one of the main eight colours listed earlier, which are repeated in sequence down the twenty-four vertebrae of the spinal column. In this way, any vibrations from an individual vertebra are picked up and interpreted to reveal where the colour balance is upset.

Once the balance or imbalance has been established, the practitioner will know which colours are required for effective treatment. Treatment involves the beaming of different coloured lights onto the patient by a special colour therapy instrument. Sometimes the whole body is bathed in the healing light, and at other times the colour will be focused only on a specific part of the body, depending on the patient's condition. The main colour used in the healing will usually be interspersed with a complementary colour, apparently increasing the efficacy of the former.

A session of this treatment will usually last around twenty minutes, and the patient should undergo at least seven or eight sessions over several weeks in order to receive the full beneficial effects. In addition to this formulaic treatment, the practitioner will advise the patient on what colours to wear and use around the home in the form of furnishings or lighting. Self-help techniques will also be taught and encouraged, to reinforce psychologically the benefits of the colour treatment. The therapist will guide the patient by visualisation exercises, which he or she may then practised at home. These exercises may include visualising a particular colour penetrating the body and suffusing it with coloured light, or the visualisation could be based on a narrative and involve the patient imagining he or she is on a journey through fields of specifically coloured flowers.

There is no doubt that colour can indeed affect mood and perhaps alter behaviour patterns, but the curative powers of colour therapy are yet to be scientifically proven. Even colour therapists recognise that this form of treatment should not replace orthodox medical diagnosis and treatment, but should be complementary.

Healing with crystals

Crystals and gemstones can be used to aid healing when used in conjunction with other alternative therapies, particularly colour therapy because of the obvious links of colour and refracted light. Some people believe that crystals are actually the tools of healing and can be used in isolation, although practices of meditation and visualisation are usually also employed. As with the previous two therapies, crystals act on energy vibrations and are believed to emit their own vibrations, which amplify and focus the natural energies of the recipient's mind and body.

Crystals are believed to alleviate blockages in the flow of energy around the body, which may be causing physical or spiritual distress. It achieves this by working on the chakra points.

The chakra is a concept of Indian origin, literally meaning wheel, and its system is used in many different types of healing. The chakras are subtle points of focused energy in the human being and are believed to be the source of physical, mental, emotional and spiritual energy. They are sometimes described in physical terms as whirling vortices that can easily become blocked, but, of course, this is merely a symbolic representation of an abstract concept.

There are seven major chakras, each relating to different functions of the mind and body. Each chakra also relates to specific colours and different gemstones. Here are the seven chakras, beginning at the bottom of the body and working up:

1. Root or base chakra

This chakra is located at the base of the spine, near the reproductive organs. It relates to sexual activity and feelings, and links us to our basic instincts. The root chakra is associated with the elimination of waste from the system and the regeneration of cells and tissues in the body. Its colour is red, and its stones are rubies, garnets and bloodstones.

2. Abdominal or sacral chakra

This chakra relates to the digestive system and the reproductive system, as well as controlling the body's production of adrenaline. This chakra also signifies happiness and openness towards others. Its colour is orange, and its gemstones are coral, carnelian and amber.

3. Solar plexus chakra

Situated at the level of the naval, this chakra relates to the internal organs, such as the liver, spleen, pancreas and intestines. It is also to do with the intellect and communication. Its colour is yellow, and its stones include citron, topaz and yellow amber.

4. Heart chakra

This chakra is connected to the heart, circulation and immune system. It is also the centre of love and emotions. The colour of the heart chakra is green, and its corresponding stones are emeralds, jade and green tourmaline.

5. Throat chakra

Located just below the vocal chords, this chakra is connected to sound and the larynx. It is also associated with the thyroid gland and the lymphatic system. The throat chakra's colour is blue, and its stones include turquoise, sapphires and aquamarine.

6. Brow chakra

Situated between the eyebrows, this chakra relates to psychic or spiritual matters, and governs the perpetuity gland and certain parts of the brain. The brow chakra coordinates all the other chakras, and its colour is indigo, its stones being amethyst, dark sapphires and lapis lazuli.

7. Crown chakra

This last chakra is located at the top of the head and is associated with the functions of the brain and spiritual aspirations. Its colours are violet and white-gold, and its stones include amethyst, rose quartz, clear crystal quartz and diamonds.

In order to unblock a chakra, a charged crystal is held above or placed directly on the area where the affected chakra is located.

There are different ways in which a crystal can be charged with energy. One method is to sit quietly holding it in your palm, concentrating on positive thoughts and visualising spiritual energy entering into it. Some people like to sleep with a crystal under their pillow, so that they can absorb their own special psychic power during dream sleep.

Another popular method of charging is to leave the crystal in direct sunlight (or moonlight) for at least six hours, or, even better, leave it outside during an electric thunderstorm.

Once a crystal has been used for healing it will have absorbed a lot of negative energy and must be cleansed before being recharged. An easy way of cleansing a crystal is to leave it to soak overnight in a bowl of spring water and sea salt, or, if there is a handy stream nearby, just give it a good dip.

When it comes to choosing a crystal, as well as bearing in mind what function you wish the stone to fulfil, you must use your intuition to guide you to what you are looking for. If you feel towards a particular stone, pick it up and handle it to see if you can sense its energy. Always inspect every crystal carefully for chips or cracks, as any imperfection may result in a dramatic loss of energy and healing sensitivity.

Here is a small selection of some of the most widely available stones and their uses:

Quartz crystal

Quartz crystal is the most easily recognizable type of healing crystal. It is the rough-cut clear stone that you will find in most New Age boutiques. Quartz is highly suitable for healing as it is believed to unblock the energy centres, allowing the body to respond and heal itself. It is a good all-round crystal to use for meditative and healing purposes as it promotes mental and spiritual well-being.

Rose quartz

Rose quartz is a beautifully coloured version of clear quartz, with its soft pink glow. This is another very important stone of healing as it deals with love and emotions. It is also a comforting stone and can ease distress in someone who has suffered trauma, as well as relieving everyday stresses and tensions.

Amethyst

Amethyst is thought to be a highly spiritual stone, associated with heightened perception and psychic insight. It is believed to have protective properties and is therefore a good stone to carry about with you. Amethyst is also said to relieve insomnia and provoke inspired dreams if placed under the pillow.

Carnelian

Of a warm red colour, this stone is believed to help with circulatory problems. Carnelian can also help to ease feelings of anger and frustration, and induce contentment and fulfilment.

Sodalite

Sodalite is a blue stone often speckled with white. It is believed to help those suffering from neuroses and irrational thoughts by balancing the mind and lowering the blood pressure.

Tiger's-eye

This also belongs to the quartz family and is golden brown in colour. Tiger's-eye is thought to increase confidence and reduce nervousness. On a physical level it can aid the digestive system.

There is no harm in experimenting with crystal in order to find out what feels right for you. Meditation with crystals is a good way to introduce yourself to the types of energy emitted, before trying to achieve healing effects. It must also be stressed that using crystals can neither diagnose illness nor provide miracle cures. If in doubt, see a doctor.

Reiki

Reiki is a Japanese form of healing that is becoming increasingly popular in this country. This healing system contains elements of just about every other alternative healing practice under the sun – spiritual healing, auras, crystals, chakra balancing, meditation, aromatherapy, naturopathy, and homeopathy.

The word *Reiki* translates as 'universal life energy', and like the preceding trio of therapies it deals with forces that are not immediately intelligible to the human senses. The essence of Reiki energy is love, 'an all-embracing divine vibration'.

Reiki energy has several basic effects: it brings about deep relaxation; destroys energy blockages; detoxifies the system; provides new vitality in the form of healing universal life energy; and increases the vibrational frequency of the body.

The laying on of hands is used in Reiki therapy, as in spiritual healing when a healer, or a person strong with life energy, places his or her hands just above a particular part of the recipient's body in order to release energy into it. The difference between Reiki and spiritual healing is that, rather than the healing sending out energy, the recipient draws it in. In this way the individual takes responsibility for his or her own healing, identifying specific needs and catering to them.

The implementation of Reiki therapy is a fairly ritualised affair. Before beginning treatment and after removing jewellery and washing the hands, the healer will perform an invocation in prayer form as a gesture of respect towards the person to whom the reiki energy will be channelled. The Reiki therapist focuses on and centres his or her own life force energy before moving on to the next ritual.

The next ritual is the smoothing out of the aura, which the therapist does with the right hand while placing the left hand on his or her abdomen. The healer strokes down the middle of the body in a fluid motion, with the hand held around twenty centimetres from the recipient's body. This can be repeated several times. This ritual establishes contact between the two people's energy fields and prepares the client for healing.

There are specific hand positions involved in Reiki treatment, all of which have a particular significance to different parts of the body and different energy centres. It is not necessary to employ the exact positioning, as Reiki energy can be drawn into any part of the body.

The first basic position is with the hands on the front of the head, covering forehead and eyes. This positioning relieves chronic diseases of every type, as well as combating stress, fatigue, allergies, weakness of will and discontentment.

When the hands are placed on the back of the head, the client can obtain relief from colds, headaches, eye problems, asthma and nausea.

The positioning of the hands on the body are numerous and can relieve all manner of ailments, from diabetes and indigestion to depression and fear of heights.

There are also several special positions that are used in the treatment of specific illnesses, such as arthritis, multiple sclerosis and heart disease.

Reiki can also be used in conjunction with the chakras (*see* Crystal healing). In this case the hands are held above a chakra that requires unblocking, and energy is absorbed into the invisible vortex, dissolving the blockage. How's that for psychic plumbing!

Meditation forms an important part of Reiki, as it encourages the individual to cease resisting and allow life and energy to flow along their chosen course. A simple meditation exercise to help you to focus on the energy within the body and the true self is to sit on the floor with your legs drawn up, soles of the feet pressed together, and hands held, palms together, at the level of the heart. It is believed that in this position the circuit of energy around the body is complete, and the chakras are aligned and open. Concentrating on this energy flow will help you to reach a state of heightened awareness.

Reiki's healing of physical disorders is only a small part of its spiritual possibilities. Accepting reiki energy enables people to live more consciously and to develop their capacity for life and love.

Chapter 7

Eastern Healing Philosophies

Many people today, disillusioned with the perceived spiritual and moral bankruptcy of contemporary western society, are turning to more ancient cultures for inspiration and enlightenment.

Eastern religions and philosophies, such as Buddhism, seem to embody the New Age tenets of personal development and psychic attunement, while offering a more appealingly mystical alternative to traditional western forms of organised religion.

These philosophies encourage new ways of viewing oneself and others, creating a deeper level of insight and self-understanding in daily life. Their emphasis on relating to others more positively through increased self-awareness provides a welcome antidote to our increasingly competitive and self-centred society in which people are fuelled by personal ambition and materialism.

Most eastern cultures embrace the concept of karma, a system of belief whereby everything that an individual does and says has a 'karmic value' that will be repaid to that person in the future. Good actions will therefore be rewarded by good fortune, and wrong actions will eventually have bad consequences on the original perpetrator.

This belief is similar to the Christian doctrine of 'love your neighbour as you love yourself', and is illustrated in the true, if slightly twee, adage 'The smile you send out will come back to you'.

The influence of the East on Western culture is already perceptible and will continue to gain ground for as long as people continue to question the existing value system and to welcome positive change.

For those in search of healing, incorporating elements of eastern philosophy into daily life can be highly beneficial. The new perspective on life and the teaching of awareness and acceptance can help to ease inner tension and induce wellbeing.

This, combined with the effects of stress-reducing techniques such as meditation, can provide effective treatment for many problems, such as depression, anxiety and phobias.

Such a state of mental, physical and spiritual attunement can also be beneficial in the treatment of more organic illnesses, as it eliminates conflict within the system, creating a state of harmony and receptivity. This, in turn, can boost the immune system, increase tolerance to pain and improve responsiveness to medication, all of which will help the healing process.

It is important, however, to emphasise that embracing these philosophies should not mean rejecting orthodox medicine. As with other alternative healing therapies, the watchword is 'complementary', and any treatment should be combined with medical consultations.

It is also important to stress that these kinds of philosophies, which focus on self-enlightenment, are not forms of psychotherapy and cannot provide easy relief from mental or emotional turmoil. In fact, the level of self-confrontation involved would make these techniques unsuitable for anyone with real psychological problems.

Buddhism

Buddhism is an ancient philosophy founded by Gautama Buddha in the sixth century BC in India, from where it was taken to China in 520 AD by a monk named Bodhidharma. It still flourishes as a practised religion in Asia, particularly in the Far East, and has elicited much interest in recent years amongst westerners searching for self-knowledge and inner tranquillity.

It could be said that of all the recognised religions practised today, Buddhism is the one that most embodies the healing ethic, as the ideal of 'wholeness' as we have come to understand it. The central teachings of Buddhism are concerned with exactly the ideas that are the mainstay of spiritual healing, in that it seeks to give its followers a new understanding of life through peace of mind.

Buddhism aims to eliminate the general feelings of dissatisfaction that pervade many people's lives, causing distress and, perhaps, illness.

Its teachings hinge on the 'noble truth' that life is unsatisfactory and engenders inescapable suffering. This inherent unsatisfactoriness is called 'dukkha', a word that suggests restlessness and suffering. Dukkha manifests itself in the individual as a kind of thirst for selfish desire, which is linked with ignorance, greed and hatred.

This belief in the inevitability of strife and suffering may sound negative and extremely pessimistic, but it is also believed that the individual is capable of achieving a state in which no selfish desire arises. As it is the unfulfilment of selfish desires that make one's life unsatisfactory, an absence of these desires leads to an acceptance of the world as it is.

In order to achieve this state of 'no dukkha', one must follow certain moral and spiritual disciplines, which are laid down in the Noble Eightfold Path.

The Noble Eightfold Path

1 Right understanding – here one acknowledges life as it is, in all its impermanence and unsatisfactoriness.
2 Right thought – this involves realising the power of one's mind, which should be filled with positive thoughts of loving-kindness and compassion.
3 Right speech – this includes not telling lies or saying anything that could be harmful to another, such as gossip.

4 Right action – such action as not taking life, stealing or engaging in sexual misconduct.
5 Right livelihood – one must be careful to have a job that does not involve one in destroying life or hurting others.
6 Right effort – this is needed in order to think about what one does and says.
7 Right awareness – one must be entirely alert or awake in life.
8 Right concentration – this is required to achieve a deeper level of attentiveness, characterised by peace and calm.

As you can see, each of the eight stages must be 'right', which means appropriate or effective. Through this 'rightness', the practising of an ethical lifestyle and meditation, the Buddhist hopes to find insight into the nature of existence and to transcend suffering.

As stressed before, this state of acceptance is not a resigned or indifferent one but a joyful one. Similarly, being without dukkha is not simply a passive, but a positive, dynamic state of contentment and compassion.

Indeed, compassion is fundamental to a Buddhist way of life. Alongside the emphasis on personal development, concern for other people and for life is paramount. A Buddhist develops 'mindfulness', starting with greater consciousness of oneself, one's body, mind and emotions, and radiating out to other people and the surrounding environment.

Meditation plays a vital role in developing mindfulness and is an important part of a Buddhist's daily routine. Meditation can take many forms and is a key factor in many healing therapies, as it encourages relaxation as well as self-awareness. (*See* the following passage on Zen for more details of Buddhist meditation techniques.)

Buddhism is a non-doctrinal religion that does not require its teachings to be forced upon its followers – its main concern is in the quest to help people achieve a full and aware life. So, in a sense, it is a philosophy that allows you to pick and choose the attitudes and practices that you wish to incorporate into your own life. Followers claim that through the teachings of the Buddha they find a special, personal path that will eventually lead them to realise their own enlightenment.

This kind of understanding transcends the intellectual and reaches deep into the self, a profound experience that leads to complete freedom.

Zen

Zen is a branch of Buddhism introduced into Japan in the twelfth century, where it has thrived ever since. Zen is a system of sustained discipline and meditation aimed at transforming the everyday experience of its followers through the traditional Buddhist teachings of insight and self-awareness. Where Zen differs from Buddhism is in its anti-rational approach, with more of an emphasis on *zazen* (meditation) and direct experience without conscious reasoning.

Zen meditation is geared towards gaining direct insight into oneself at a level too deep to be expressed in words. This kind of transcendental meditation leads to enlightenment. As in other forms of Buddhism, Zen also teaches that accepting the world as it is and abandoning selfish desires are essential steps in the quest for enlightenment.

This acquiescence to the 'unsatisfactoriness', instability and impermanence of life, as described in the earlier section on Buddhism, reaches out into every aspect of life, including self-identity. A sense of a fixed personal identity is seen to be illusory, as everything on earth is impermanent and mutable, including the 'self'. Zen teaching therefore concentrates on encouraging the individual to discard any established self-image or notion of ego, thereby acknowledging and embracing the transience of existence. With each moment of insight, the influence exerted by the personal 'I' on the individual's way of thinking lessens and a new, more profound understanding develops.

This kind of understanding is cultivated through the use of three main techniques: daily life practice, meditation, and anecdotal wisdom.

Daily life practice

The aim is to live your life according to the Buddhist principle of 'mindfulness', which means being continually aware of all your own actions and responses. Again, this entails adhering to the Noble Eightfold Path and releasing yourself from preconceptions and driving desires, thus quashing the wilful, self-serving side of the personality. In this state, happiness and suffering are equally gratefully received as part of the ever-changing pattern of life.

Meditation

The Zen form of meditation, known as zazen, is really a way of perfecting daily-life practice. It encourages 'stillness' and 'mindfulness', eventually enabling the meditator to carry thought beyond the limits of the intellect by allowing thoughts to come and go freely, without making judgements on them. Ultimately, the person reaches a state of heightened awareness, without the intrusion of a personal 'I' who is aware.

The practising of zazen is slightly ritualised – the meditator always sits cross-legged on a cushion, with the back absolutely straight, head upright, and the centre of gravity completely aligned so that weight is evenly distributed around the body.

Many meditative exercises centre on concentrating on one's own breathing, and the simplest Zen meditation focuses on this principle. The meditator silently counts each exhalation of breath. The idea is to count from one up to ten without any other thoughts crossing the mind. When a thought does arise, the sitter must expel it and restart the count from one.

Trying this at home will show you just how hard it is to free the mind from rational interjecture, but if you persevere you will also begin to discover the profound states of calm that can be experienced.

Zen practitioners meditate daily, either privately or in groups, and the duration of a meditative session can be infinitely variable.

Anecdotal wisdom

One of the more notorious elements of Zen philosophy is its subscription to the use of symbolic stories, riddles and paradoxes. There are usually no firm conclusions to be drawn from these stories through contemplation, rather the wisdom comes from accepting that there is no right answer. These puzzles confront the intellect with a wall that no amount of logical reasoning can surmount. The hope is that intuitive insight will take over and instinctively offer a response 'born of the immediate moment' – a smile, an exclamation, the sight of an otter shaking itself, the sound of the wind in the trees – moments of experience that intrinsically define existence. The answer is, in a sense, to un-ask the question and to realise that the problem rests in calling it a problem. Probably the best-known example of a Zen puzzle is: 'What is the sound of one hand clapping?'

If you wish to expand your mind and heighten your awareness through this particular philosophy, you must find a good teacher, as Zen is taught as a form of apprenticeship. Most major cities in Britain now have some form of Buddhist Society, where you will be able to receive information about finding a teacher in your area. For further information *see* Useful Addresses.

Hinduism – the Ayurvedic system

In Indian society there are many practitioners of Ayurvedic medicine, an ancient Hindu system of healing based on both natural and homoeopathic remedies. It uses mental techniques actually to alter bodily responses to disease processes – a form of 'mind over matter'. This system also involves concentration on primordial sounds, such as meaningless syllabic sounds, or mantras. The patient repeats these sounds unceasingly for long periods of time in order to concentrate the mind and focus attention away from pain. These techniques are often used in conjunction with transcendental meditation for general improvement of wellbeing.

Ayurveda is a complete system of healing that deals with every aspect of an individual's physical, mental and spiritual health. In the language of Ayurveda, these three aspects are known as the physical, the subtle and the causal, and 'health' is defined as a harmonious functioning of all three together.

The name 'Ayurveda' comprises two Sanskrit words, *ayur*, meaning 'life' or 'daily living', and *veda*, meaning 'knowledge'. Ayurveda, therefore, is the knowledge of daily living, meaning that it is a medical system that emphasises an understanding of Nature and the individual's place within society and the universe. This emphasis on the *individual* is key to the Ayurvedic system, which is more a whole lifestyle than simply a set of treatments. An Ayurvedic practitioner will keep in close contact with his or her patient, monitoring and assessing the patient's entire way of life – diet, exercise, habits, sleep patterns, religious beliefs, occupation and conditions at work, state of personal relationships, and so on. By finding out all he or she can about the patient's personal and professional life, eating habits and medical history, the therapist can advise changes as necessary in order to prevent the onset of illness.

One of the most important teachings in the

Ayurvedic diagnosis of a patient is the Tridosha theory. According to Ayurvedic law, everyone and everything in the universe is comprised of three basic elements or 'doshas'. These three doshas are called vata, pitta and kapha and are said to control all mental and physical processes. The nature of each dosha can be likened to the forces of the wind, the sun and the moon.

Vata

This is compared to the wind and is the moving force behind the other two doshas, which are believed to be immobile without it. Because of this, vata is considered to be the most influential of the Tridosha. It is responsible for all the body's actions and sensations, controlling the central nervous system and the respiratory and circulatory systems. It also regulates thought processes, promoting mental balance and comprehension.

Pitta

This is comparable to the sun and is a source of heat and energy. The word 'pitta' literally means 'that which digests things', and this dosha governs the digestive system, the metabolism, and all biochemical processes in the body. It is also re-

sponsible for the 'digestion' of ideas and perceptions, stimulating the intellect and the capacity for
curiosity and enthusiasm.

Kapha

This is likened to the moon, with its tidal influence. Kapha controls the balance of fluids in the
body and governs cell growth and structure. In
fact, it provides support and structure for the
whole body, giving strength and stability, both
physical and psychological. Kapha also stimu-
lates the capacity for positive emotions such as
love, peace, patience and courage.

Every individual consists of a combination of
these three basic forces in differing proportions.
Their relative proportions in a person is thought to
be determined at conception and continues
throughout childhood and adult life. Good health
results when all three doshas are working in harmony, with none exerting any more considerable
force than the others. In his or her diagnosis,
therefore, the Ayurvedic physician must first try
to identify and understand the patient's inborn
disposition. This he or she does through examination of the patient's eyes, skin, hair, nails, tongue,

spittle, urine and stools. The practitioner will also listen carefully to the voice and take note of physical mannerisms and general physique. By all these means he or she can establish a person's basic constitution and identify which dosha 'rules' the individual's body.

Characteristics of the vata individual

Vata people have thin, bony bodies and dry, rough skin. The hair is also thin and dry, and often curly. Their eyes are small and dull, often dark in colour, and their teeth tend to be large and prone to decay. The voice is weak, hoarse and uncertain. Psychologically, these people are creative, active and intellectually sharp.

Characteristics of the pitta individual

Pitta people are of medium height and build, with reddish complexions and oily skin. Their hair is soft, fine and fair, light brown or red. The eyes are sharp and penetrating, often green or grey in colour, and teeth are medium sized and yellowish. The voice tends to be sharp and high-pitched. These people are highly intelligent, with strong leadership qualities.

Characteristics of the kapha individual

Kapha people have large, strong physiques, with a tendency to be overweight. The skin is pale and smooth, and the hair is thick, dark and wavy. They have large, attractive eyes, often blue, and large white teeth. The voice is clear, deep and well-pitched. These people learn slowly but have long memories, and their thoughts are generally logical and well-considered.

Obviously, these are purist manifestations of different dosha types, and one would not be likely to encounter an individual with all the characteristics of a particular dosha, as everyone is a combination of all three types, and where one type is dominant the other two doshas will serve to modify it.

Once the practitioner has assessed the dosha type, he or she will be able to pinpoint any imbalance that may cause distress or disease and will treat the patient accordingly. As Ayurveda has a strong doctrine of prevention, people are often treated before showing any signs of illness. If, however, illness does occur, a wide variety of treatments is available – from conventional surgery to plant-derived drugs.

Basic treatments fall into three main categories: medicinal, practical and dietary.

Medicinal remedies

There are some 8,000 different medicines designed to heal patients, made from natural substances such as herbs, vegetables and minerals. Each drug is custom-blended to create the right balance of ingredients for the individual patient. In addition, various orthodox medicines and treatments may be prescribed by the Ayurvedic physician.

Practical remedies

These include complementary therapies such as massage, yoga, oil treatments, breathing exercises and meditation. These practices are prescribed in order to promote general wellbeing as well as to treat physical and psychological disorders.

Dietary discipline

Foods are broken down into six types: sweet, sour, salty, pungent, bitter and astringent. A patient is prescribed different types of food according to his or her individual needs. Food is also prepared and consumed in accordance with external factors, such as time of year, time of day and weather conditions. It is also important that food is fully savoured, well chewed and swallowed in a relaxed, contented state of mind.

Most Ayurvedic practitioners qualify first in orthodox medicine and then attend courses in Ayurveda, so professional integrity is ensured. There are some 60 to 70 orthodox doctors practising Ayurvedic medicine in Britain. For further information *see* Helpful Addresses or ask your GP.

Many Western doctors agree that Ayurveda is a highly effective health-care system, with its emphasis on preventative measures and physical, mental and spiritual wellbeing.

Sufism

Sufism is an Islamic mystical movement originating in Persia in the seventh century AD as a reaction against what the Sufis perceived as the increasing worldliness and rigidity of orthodox Islam. The orthodox rejected them at first, but today Sufi orders are fully accepted among the majority Islamic groups.

It is difficult to define clearly the distinction between Sufism and Islam, as both are contained within each other. In a way Sufism is at the heart of Islam. The Sufis aim to remain true and pure in the following of the teachings of Islam but to concentrate particularly on the idea of inner awakening, and to explore consciousness through the understanding of the relationship between the inner and outer life. Shaykh Fadhlella Haeri describes the key to Sufism as 'that of inner awakening, freedom and joy through recognition of outer restriction by choice and discrimination'. The practices of genuine Sufis result in outer discipline and inner openings and delights.

In common with most mystical traditions, the aim of the Sufi is direct experience of, and ultimately union with, God or Allah. This is achieved through ascetic practices and, more importantly, through love, both of God and of other people. Sufism has been called 'the religion of the heart', as it centres on purity of heart and feeling, relying on a largely devotional approach with the emphasis on intuition and emotion. There is no religious dogma in Sufism, nor any rigidly structured philosophical system that defines its beliefs.

Sufism stresses the ideal of equilibrium and wholeness, both in the self and in the universe. The Sufis see that the human being is potentially a microcosm of the balanced unity of the universe. The idea is not to retreat from the world by looking inwards, but to bring one's own vision and insight into the world. By gaining knowledge of God, the devotee becomes in turn a channel through which God's knowledge can act in the world.

The Sufis have always used many different methods and techniques to develop consciousness. Their practices include contemplative meditation, breathing exercises, music, visualisation and controlled movement. Meditation techniques can include repetitive mantras, such as 'La ilaha illa'llah', meaning 'There is no god but Allah'. The Sufi repeats this phrase until his or her mind is free from thought.

Sufism draws several analogies from the practising of medicine. Indeed, Sufi prophets and spiritual masters are considered to be the physicians of the soul. In fact, many Sufi masters do themselves practise medicine in order to be able to treat themselves and their immediate followers. The physical body must be in a state of calm and equilibrium in order to experience inner stillness.

Sufis are constantly striving towards harmony and right action, facilitating healing of the heart through purity and calm. The main purpose of life is seen to be awake fully, to learn the disciplines of abandonment and submission, and to discover the common uniting force behind everything.

The Sufi aims to reach the peak of his or her self, overcoming the obstacles of mind and the intellect, to become spontaneously aware of 'beingness'. Each Sufi order develops its own techniques in reaching the heights of the self. Like Buddhism, Sufism enables each individual to go on a personal journey in order to arrive at his or her own particular understanding of reality.

Obviously, becoming a follower of Sufism means fully embracing the teachings of Islam and the Koran, but there are many interesting lessons that the western spiritual traveller can learn from the study of this religion.

Chapter 8

Healing and the Occult

'The Occult' is a phrase that often provokes a negative reaction amongst those for whom it has sinister connotations. For many people, the occult conjures up associations with satanic cults and the forces of evil; subjects that, understandably, inspire fear and condemnation. Those who are interested in the practices of the occult are considered to be devil-worshipping sociopaths, intent on inflicting harm on others and invoking evil spirits.

It is true that in any section of society there are those who are going to abuse their position and act unlawfully or immorally, and the occultist community is no different. These cases, however, create a false image of the mystical arts, which have as great a capacity for good as for evil.

It is human nature to be afraid of what is unknown, and that is exactly what the occult is, its literal translation being 'that which is kept hidden'. The term covers many different disciplines, including spiritualism, paganism, white and black witchcraft, shamanism, voodoo, and more widely recognised practices such as tarot and other forms of fortune-telling.

Some people believe that it is wrong to 'dabble' in the unknown and tamper with things that are beyond our common understanding. Surely, however, it is better to strive to understand rather than remain ignorant and fearful?

It is perhaps not surprising that the world of the supernatural is particularly fascinating to those people who are interested in alternative and esoteric therapies, as both require an attitude of open-mindedness and a thirst for cosmic communion. Most importantly, they require an acceptance that there are realms of experience that cannot be explained by rational thought or scientific investigation.

The world is defined by our perceptions of it, and five has always seemed an inadequately small number of senses with which to understand such an infinite environment. It almost seems like a rational approach to acknowledge that there must be things beyond our ken, imperceptible or merely intangible. Faith healing is such a phenomenon, confounding intellect and defying explanation, and healing and occultism can be married to remarkable effect. The forces of the supernatural can be harnessed with beneficial consequence to help the sick and the troubled, if we are to believe the common reports of such cases.

One of the most significant areas of human experience that can be helped by occultist healing methods is the commonly fearful attitude towards death. The disciplines of the occult may help people to come to terms with death, their own or that of loved ones, and accept it as an inevitable part of the universe and its life cycle. For many people it is comforting to believe that there are worlds beyond our own and that death is not the end.

As with any topic of study concerning people's fundamental beliefs, investigation into the occult and its practices should not be taken on lightly, and anyone of an exceptionally superstitious or anxious nature should probably not delve too deeply into the world of the preternatural.

Witch doctors – keepers of the flame

A reason for the detachment with which doctors view the healer is the association of healing in the popular mind with occultist practices, such as seances and the activities of the witch doctor. Doctors themselves are not exempt from these popular prejudices. Yet if we take the time to examine the work of the witch doctor, we find that the Western doctor has much to learn from him. In the meeting between witch doctor and sufferer, the humanity of the patient is never disregarded. He or she does not receive the blow to one's selfdom, which is the standard in Western culture, where the patient often feels he or she has been dehumanised and reduced to the level of a simple number or case. The witch doctor would never be so crass or ignorant. This kind of therapeutic problem is alien to tribal medicine, where the soul is considered to necessitate healing along with the body.

Our distant ancestors did not see themselves as distinct from the environment. The stars, the spirits and the gods that controlled the cosmos also controlled the people. Human beings were intimately involved with nature. Shamans and medicine men use prayers, chants, talismans, herbs and potions to influence a world that humans in primitive society could not understand or influence. Faith healing of a simple kind is present still in so-called 'backward' parts of the world where medical science has made few inroads. The therapeutic powers of the local witch doctor are boosted by the implicit belief in the potency of his magic in the community. From centuries of observation and experiment, he has developed a pharmacopoeia for everyday needs, such as inducing vomiting in the case of poison; purgatives for ridding children of worms; sedatives for quieting hysterics; and potions for chest colds, headaches, whooping cough, dysentery, snakebite, swellings, and stings. If his remedies were all totally ineffective, the medicine man would soon lose his standing in the community, just as a doctor would in ours. The witch doctor's remit is to deal with a multiplicity of illnesses – sudden fevers, barrenness in women – and to help the community cope with the sudden death of a chief. The pharmaceutical knowledge of witch doctors has often preceded that of scientific medicine. Malaria was successfully treated by South American tribes prior to Old World doctors, and African Somalis diagnosed the transmission of the disease by the mosquito at least two centuries before Europeans. The modern witch doctor compares favourably with the western doctor. The comparison is especially favourable regarding illnesses of a hysterical or psychiatric nature, illnesses such as impotence and loss of speech.

A great deal of the witch doctor's treatment is psychological in essence and is in the realm of faith healing. The witch doctor flourishes in primitive societies because of the belief that good and evil govern both the spirit world and the human world. The witch doctor is on the side of the good, and his chief function is to protect the community from evil spirits. In the light of modern discoveries of the relationship between mind and body in illness, the ancient craft of the witch doctor appears surprisingly modern.

Primitive societies all over the world have their medicine men, or witch doctors. They nearly all wear colourful ceremonial costumes and use mysterious rituals to impress their suggestible patients. Native medicine is also closely bound up with the local religious cult, and involves the use of totem figures and charms to ward off sickness, which is usually attributed to evil spirits. The witch doctor is both physician, psychiatrist, chaplain and private detective. Death is rarely regarded as a natural and unavoidable event but is usually ascribed to be the work of a supernatural agency. Here the witch doctor will be required to act as a priest to decide what spirit has been affronted or abused. His capacity as private detective will be utilised, as the witch doctor must then investigate possible conspirators responsible for the illness. He is also a therapist, as part of his job is to administer herbal remedies, massage or heat treatment. He will also make ritual incantations, which will lull the patient into a state of placidity.

Many of the multicoloured ceremonial rituals, the masks and extravagant grass costumes put on by native doctors have a design. They are a visual assistance to psychiatric doctoring. Native medicine on the tribal level is almost invariably combined with psychiatry, an approach which 'civilised' practice has only newly adopted.

The visual aids, symbolic incantations and persuasive assertion used by native doctors may be regarded either as sympathetic magic or as a mild hypnotic suggestion. The doctor might say while bathing his patient: 'Your trouble is departing as this river is flowing out to sea.'

The religious mien of native psychiatry is provided by the local cult. This may entail a belief in the intercession of one of the ancestors, often recently dead, whose power as an elder is remembered. A suffering person may feel that his or her illness is accountable to the spirit of a dead uncle who beat him badly during his childhood. He will be advised to desist from the bad behaviour that has brought about this visitation from the spirit.

In parts of Ghana, there is a tradition of the use of deep hypnosis by witch doctors, who may induce a trance in a roomful of patients at a time. Authorised observers claim that the Ghanaian native doctors are able to cure serious skin disorders by this spiritual method.

The shaman

A shaman is said to use healing energies either to heal or to harm. These powers are used to maintain the order of the community. 'Voodoo' or 'hexing' has long been associated in many cultures with healing. The term 'shaman' is derived

from the Tunguso-Manchurian term *saman*,
which means 'he who knows'. In taking their professional vows, healers vow to harm as well as
heal in their society in order to maintain order.
Shamans of Siberian, Eskimo and American Indian tribes were initiated into their tribes not by
their mastery of an arcane body of knowledge but
by personally imposed ordeals. These ordeals
would involve fasting and experiencing visions
induced by trances. After this initiation the shaman would be credited with many abilities, such
as healing and access to divine revelation.

The Indian shaman is said to be able to cure
snakebites by methods akin to those employed by
the Africans. Many Indian snakebites are not poi-
sonous, but the shock of the bite can be so severe
that it can be lethal to a suggestible person ignorant of this. Nobody really knows whether the
shaman cures only the state of shock, or rather increases the bodily resistance to the poison.

In Patagonian tribes the shaman, or witch doctor, held an important position. The usual treatment of the patient involved creating as much hul-
labaloo and clatter as possible to drive away the
aggressive demon. The shaman would also suck a

part of the sufferer's body and then brandish a stone, a stick or an insect that the shaman would claim had been drawn from the body of the afflicted person. Often the patient would be strapped to the back of a horse and sent out into the day amid a great tumult and uproar. As well as disquiet, cold was thought to be a great curative next to noise. If needs be, a mare would be sacrificed in the house of the sufferer. The shaman would deliver the fatal stab to the heart. The animal would writhe in convulsions as its heart was extracted. The assembled company would then feed on the horse. What was left of the unfortunate animal would be taken to a local hill top and erected on a pole. If this failed to bring about a cure, the case was considered beyond help.

White witches: 'We died of ourselves'

The nearest cousin to the witch doctor in Europe is the art of the white witch. Practice of the 'cunning arts' was common in Britain as recently as two centuries ago. White witchery was regarded as liable to cure as it was to curse. It was only about a hundred years ago that the majority of the population lived away from the towns, away from any qualified medical aid. Anyone suffering from pneumonia stood approximately the same chance of recovery three thousand years ago as they did in the mid-1930s.

In Hanoverian England, for instance, traditional medicine had not really moved decisively beyond the language and lore of the ancient world. Even the products of the Royal College of Physicians emerged from their training with scarcely more formidable diagnostic tools than their quack counterparts. Most physicians could offer little more than laudanum and sympathy.

Prior to the beginning of medical services to rural areas in 1911, folk medicine held sway among country people. The average labourer in rural England was too poor to employ the services of a doctor. The faith healers of these communities were white witches. The most renowned of the areas where white witchcraft held sway was the North of England. Here a white witch could quite openly ply her trade of magic medicines and love charms up until the middle of the 1830s. Most famous were the Wise Man of Brompton and his female counterpart the Wise Woman of Cloughton.

A number of folk remedies used in the past are

now manufactured as pharmaceutical preparations prescribed by physicians. For example, rauwolfia is an extract of the snakeroot plant, which was used in the Far East for its calming effect. It is now prescribed by physicians to lower blood pressure.

Foxglove was first brewed by Indians to treat dropsy, fluid in the legs caused by heart problems. This practice was extant centuries before it was discovered that foxglove contributed the active ingredients now known as digitalis, a treatment now employed to stimulate weakened hearts.

Folk medicine is still popular among large groups of Mexican-Americans in New Mexico, Colorado, Arizona, California, and especially in west Texas. Their healing system is based on pre-Columbian indigenous lore, and its popularity reflects the isolation of Mexican-Americans from mainstream American culture and the unwillingness of Mexican-Americans to assimilate to Anglo-Saxon culture. Prominent among Mexican-American faith healers is the *curandero*, a type of shaman who uses white magic and herbs to effect cures. In the cosmic struggle between good and evil, the curandero, using God-given powers,

wards off harmful spells and hexes. As in other
faith healing practices, the essence of the success
of the curandero lies in the patient's faith in his
abilities.

Spiritualism

The spiritualist movement began in 1848 in a
house in Hydesville, New York State, where lived
the Fox sisters, Leah, Margeretta and Kate. At
first the whole family were disturbed by
'paranormal' happenings such as phantoms and
bizarre unexplained knockings. The parents decided that an unquiet spirit was to blame, and two
of the sisters, Margeretta and Kate, began a communication with the spirit. They were on the way
to fame and becoming celebrated figures. The
only drawback is that in 1888 the two sisters who
had been principal in the occurrences, Margeretta
and Kate, admitted that they had faked these alter-
cations with the afterlife. But by then it was too
late. The spiritualist church that they founded
continued unabashed. Spirit healing is a branch of
this minority religion, a branch that now over-
shadows the original movement as a church.

Generally thought of as being interested purely

in communication with the spirit world, the spiritualist church has developed a growing interest in
healing, confirmed when, in 1963, the National
Federation of Spiritual Healing in Britain boasted
of having over two thousand practitioners.

Spiritualists believe that in their work they are
merely facilitating the Christian belief in the divine power of healing. Spiritual healing is distinct
from faith healing in one important aspect. In
faith healing, what is paramount is the patient's
personal belief. In the case of spiritual healing,
however, faith itself is irrelevant, and the source
of the power is said to emanate from the spirits of
the dead in attendance. These spirits are brought
forth by means of a spiritualist medium. Needless
to say, mediumistic or spiritist diagnosis made
through spirit guides and clairvoyance are ex-
pressly forbidden in scripture (Deuteronomy
18:9–13).

No less a person than James Joyce satirised the
pseudo-scientific language of spiritualism in that
seminal work of modernist literature, *Ulysses*. In
the Cyclops chapter, which opens in Barney
Kiernan's bar, an unnamed bibulous Dubliner re-
counts how the 'apparition of the etheric double'

during a seance is particularly lifelike 'owing to the discharge of jivic rays from the crown of the head'. Yet there was a more serious side to this. Spiritualism's most celebrated critic was the renowned escapologist, Harry Houdini. He was an unwilling participant in this personal crusade, in that nobody more than he would have liked to have believed in the afterlife. What dismayed him was the deceit and exploitation of human anguish that were employed in these sessions of communications with the dead. 'It ought to be stopped, it must be stopped,' he wrote. Distinguished figures from the world of science investigated the claims, and, in the case of Sir William Crookes, the eminent physicist, found in favour of the spiritualists.

Houdini bewailed the fact that it was only scientists who were sent to investigate the claims because the fact that these men were scientists did not ensure that they would not be immune to the extremely clever and sophisticated trickery that a spiritualist may employ. Indeed, even he, the 'Great Houdini', claimed that he himself could be deceived by the trickery of the spiritualists. If he could be fooled, a man who had devoted his life to the creation of illusion, who then was immune?

Harry Edwards

One of the most renowned faith healers in England in the 1950s was Harry Edwards. More than any other, he popularised healing to the public. On one occasion he managed to fill the Royal Albert Hall. As an amateur magician, Edwards went along to spiritualist meetings eager to expose the chicanery he felt was involved. Instead, the converse occurred and he became an initiate and disciple of the church.

He believed that his success was because of the fact that he was in communication with spirits when engaged in the healing process. These spirits, he believed, wished to help the living. His belief in these spirits meant that he was attended by a guide, or medium, during his healing sessions. Edwards was himself a convert to spiritualism and claimed he was in contact with the spirits of Louis Pasteur and Lord Lister.

It is a matter of documented fact that Edwards treated individuals who then made dramatic recoveries. Possibly this is merely because of the fact that he treated a very large number of sick people, and in the light of this it seems only a matter of statistics that some of the people that he treated would make dramatic recoveries, just as there will always be dramatic recoveries amongst a percentage of a number of the sick.

Edward's success and notoriety were felt to have sufficient weight and theological import for the Archbishop of Canterbury to set up a special commission in 1958 to investigate the evidence for spiritual healing. It concluded, predictably, that there was no evidence of any supernatural healing power at work with spiritualist mediums. Whatever one's views on the subject, one could hardly expect such a deeply conservative or-ganisation as the Church of England to find in favour of the spiritualists, whatever evidence was proffered. Edwards continued healing until his death.

Chapter 9

Roles of the Healer

Who are they?

Over the centuries the qualifications for being a faith healer have been as bizarre and as arbitrary as they can be. It was once believed that husbands and wives with the same surname before marriage had healing powers. Another prime candidate for healing power was a baby born with a membrane over its head. Just as the Catholic church will limit the practice of formal exorcism to well-chosen and judicious priests with the express permission of a bishop, the ability to heal in particularly gifted individuals will grudgingly be accepted by the church. The gift of healing is like many other gifts – some people will have a natural aptitude for it that marks them out.

Having been the recipient of healing, you may want to investigate the possibility of being a healer yourself. To this end I have enclosed a few useful addresses at the back of the book. The distribution of the healing ability does not seem to favour one class over another. As with anything, practice will enhance ability, but ultimately how successful one is will be dependent on one's natural ability. Mystics, faith healers and gurus, like great painters and musicians, have to go through a long and disciplined developmental stage, as a sense of the spiritual is not enough to sustain them.

A large number of healers begin as one-time patients of healers, and to their astonishment they are told that they themselves have the healing ability. St Paul makes it clear that only some are given the ability to heal (1 Corinthians 12:9). Yet in the Gospel of Mark, Jesus says: 'Everything is possible for anyone who has faith' (Mark 9:32b).

Any would-be healer has to resolve the moral dilemma that he or she may be hurting people by giving them false hopes. This probably explains why healers have to enter the field with strong personal convictions and the tentative first steps of Arigo and the Stroker. One can have an innate capacity to 'feel' illness and diagnose it through one's hands. What is reassuring is that if someone does have the gift of healing it will not be long before it is recognised. Sometimes it may be intuitively felt by others that you have the healing gift.

During the course of writing this book, I embarked on a series of driving lessons. On mentioning to my driving instructor that I was writing this epic on the subject of faith healing, he said, 'Well, I've got a story for you.' He proceeded to tell me that after sustaining a twisted ankle from a fall down a pothole he was wracked by pains in his ankle for weeks. It transpired he had twisted a ligament.

One night, about a month after this, he was putting his four-year-old daughter Rebecca to bed. He decided to ask his daughter to lay her hand on the offending ankle and pray to Jesus to heal him. The pain then disappeared without ceremony. He found he could walk around and run up and down stairs untroubled by pain in a way he hadn't done for weeks.

This man lived on the same street as me, the street where I had grown up. It became clear to me then that healing was in fact alive and well and not consigned to some hazy Biblical past. Alive in a quiet, unassuming way in the lives of ordinary people, not in some dramatic or ostentatious way. If one only stops to consider it, everyone has met individuals whose physical presence was commanding in some inexpressible manner, either by sheer physicality or force of intellect. Some may even have felt a corresponding feeling that they would, if asked, bend to the will of that person, whatever they were to ask. Yet if asked to articulate precisely why this was the case, I think that most people would be unable to do so. Everyone can recognise the 'aura' another person, perhaps even a stranger, is giving off without a word of communication between them. Some people can leave you feeling weary while others can leave you feeling inspired and revivified. It is a short leap from this to imagine the presence and ambience of the healer.

Even the most imperceptive can recognise a baleful or beautiful aura on a wordless, pre-verbal level. It is interesting that when we attempt to discuss this phenomenon, we are drawn inevitably into using a vocabulary that centres on the idea of energy and energy fields, words such as 'electric' and 'vibrations' being the most obvious examples. Perhaps this is a clue to what passes between the healer and recipient during a session, the healer projecting some positive high-intensity energy into the recipient.

The universality of healing suggests its deep resonance and significance to us. As we have seen, faith healing's resonance is multicultural and transcontinental. It has been present in some form in the Graeco-Roman world, the Indic culture of the East, on the African continent, in the Americas, and in the former Soviet Union. In advanced late capitalist post-modern urbane western society, particularly in America, where fundamentalist religion is very popular, huge crowds attend faith healing meetings.

When we study the archetypal faith healers (by 'archetypal' I mean figures who follow the career pattern, well established in healing, of the tentative beginning followed by rise to notoriety followed by establishment clampdown) what is perplexing and ultimately uplifting about them is their endearing guilelessness. The really successful healers tend to be unassuming souls and not even markedly religious people.

At the outset we have to distinguish here between the avaricious televangelist breed of healer and the more dignified figures of healing. This is a thorny question, but one we have to confront. The reason it is so thorny is that both types of healer can use the same methodology to achieve their ends. What may be, and what we will examine here, is that the methodology in question has a potency that the healers are unaware of themselves. Its power exists, and one can use it to good or acquisitive ends.

If we examine the classic figures of healing – the Stroker, Quimby and Arigo, for example – instead of the cynical manipulator or the charlatan, we meet the idiot savant. A prime example of this would be Valentine Greatrakes, timorously beginning his healing in fear of looking a fool to the populace and most of all his own wife.

His powers had so much of 'the extraordinariness' about them, he wrote, that 'I thought fit to conceal [them] for some time'. Jose de Freitas (Arigo) is another example of the idiot savant, displaying amazing abilities yet comically falling into a dead faint after witnessing them played back to him on film.

I use the term 'idiot' reservedly here because I do not wish to suggest that these men were imbeciles, rather that their beginnings were often clownish and instinctual rather than rationally considered. I should add a warning here, as it should be said that most healers enter the practice through strong personal conviction. These people are far from being fools, and, indeed, a person would have to be a fool to hold a mass healing in the way that Mesmer or Jacob did without some special healing gift. Often the end of the career of the healer has a resemblance to that other clownish figure, the King for a Day, as many healers also find – usually after a sustained attack on their confidence by the medical establishment – that their powers wane or completely disappear. Mesmer and Greatrakes are prime examples of this. Yet it goes without saying that if their abilities disappear, we must accept that there must have been something there in the first place.

Unexceptional in all other regards, these men confound any charge of charlatanism that may be brought against them in their very simplicity. Of course, the cynic could say that this is feigned simplicity. If one does subscribe to this view, then one has to ask to what end would a healer conduct such a masquerade?. Healers run huge risks. Nine white witches were executed at Husband's Bosworth in the Midlands for failing to effect a cure against epilepsy. Today, if they become big enough to rock the boat of orthodox medicine they can still be imprisoned. In 1981, a German healer called Joseph Muller was imprisoned for two years in West Germany. He was found guilty of 'contravention of the laws governing medical practice'.

Neither can we see healing as the gulling of one class by another. Faith healers and the people that heal come from any and every class. We have aristocratic faith healers, such as the Earl of Sandwich and Prince Alexander von Hohenlohe. Then there are the peasant healers, such as the Cheshire woman Bridget Bostock and Arigo. Nobody is compelled to believe in the faith healer, yet millions of people use their services. The German philosopher Schopenhauer writes that 'Belief is like love; and as any attempt to compel love produces hate, so it is the attempt to compel belief that first produces real unbelief.' (Essays and Aphorisms). In the face of this we must ask why faith healing persists and continues to fascinate a cynical public. The intellectual accessibility of the ideas, which would attempt to explain healing to the man on the street, is another factor that could account for the popularity of healing, and this contrasts sharply with the Latinate and obscure language of the doctor. The notion that good health can be seen as the balancing of energies within the body is eminently plausible to the layman, who probably knows that his pancreas and liver perform actions akin to this in their regulatory function. The complexities of biochemical changes within the body and physiology may be off-putting, but the healer's art is graspable. Aiding this is the healer's primary wish to communicate with the patient in a meaningful manner, a revolutionary sentiment yet to storm the medical profession.

Perhaps there are socio-biological reasons for the magnetism of the healer. There is a deepseated need in human beings to want to submit themselves to a dominant member of the group in which they live, inherited from our monkey and ape ancestors. This must in some part explain the attraction of the healer and the witch doctor. The healer provides answers and confidence in an uncertain world. The witch doctor is a particularly salient example as he is often second only to the tribal chief in his society.

Yet more than this, the figure of the healer will occupy a number of deeply resonant roles that play to our inner psyche. We cannot view the healer as merely a kind of glorified doctor with some added mysticism thrown in for good luck. It would also be inappropriate to associate the role of a doctor with the role of the healer, as the healer's role embraces much more than the doctor's. Whereas in the West the roles of doctor and counsellor are divorced, the healer acts as both these figures and more.

Healer as lover

The psychoanalyst Carl Jung (1875–1961) wrote: 'Christ the healer is one of the eternal images or archetypes.' The healer is a tremendously potent figure in our imaginations. We have said that the witch doctor is both physician, psychiatrist, chaplain and private detective. The faith healer, his western cousin, can also boast a variety of functions. He or she is the lover, employing touch in a therapeutic way that it is difficult to imagine any doctor or counsellor ever contemplating. One cannot underestimate the potency and the primacy of touch. Embryos react to touch at just six weeks. The first contact with the external world the baby will experience will be through the medium of touch. By extension, spending 50 minutes a week with someone who is touching you and making eye contact with you, and is fully involved with you and your illness is a tremendously positive and invigorating experience. It would be a lucky patient indeed who received 50 minutes (or even 5 minutes!) of a doctor's time today. Moreover, a patient in the care of a doctor will no doubt meet different doctors from the one he or she originally saw on follow-up visits. Yet with healers there is a sense of continuity built up, which strengthens the confidence of the patient.

This demonstrates that sometimes the success of a healer can lie in quite prosaic answers. If you were an old lady living alone in a high-rise block, the very act of being physically touched and spoken to sensitively and softly with a healer's undivided attention would be therapeutic.

It has been found that one of the most compel-

ling figures to the female psyche is that of the
mysterious stranger, a figure that Emily Brontë
used as a key motif in drawing the character of
Heathcliff, perhaps the greatest romantic hero in
all English literature. Like Heathcliff and the By-
ronic hero, the healer is handsome, magnetic and
melancholy. We are also slightly ambivalent
about him. Consciously or unconsciously, the
healer taps into the resonance of this figure.

To put it less discreetly, we should not ignore
the factor of sex as an element in the appeal of the
healer. Mutual attraction was undoubtedly there
between Baker Eddy and Phineas Quimby. No
doubt it explains the appeal of a figure like
Rasputin, who obviously possessed strong sexual
magnetism, and clearly it was an element in the
attraction of the female genteel society that sur-
rendered their dignity to Mesmer. Striking good
looks and personal magnetism also play a part in
the appeal of Djuna Davitashvili.

Modern healers tend to have a disproportion-
ately high number of female patients. A wander
around any complementary health fair shows a
preponderance of women over men. Two-thirds of
pilgrims to Lourdes are women. A possible expla-

nation for this is that women tend to have far less control over their lives than men and are therefore more inclined to believe in an external force over which they have no control, be it healing, horoscopes or magic crystals.

Mystery and mastery

This also ties in with another important element in the psychology of faith healing, which is the weighty factor of mystery. Every general practitioner has a catalogue of twenty or so drugs that can be administered and are well known to both practitioner and patient. This tends to kill off any sense of awe or romance in the healing process. When one is attended by a healer one feels that one is taking part in an ancient mystical rite that taps into a past of folklore, of witchery bequeathed to us from remote generations past or (and perhaps more importantly) our imagined romanticised perceptions of it gleaned from television and books. This element of mystery also manages to coexist cheerfully with the intellectual accessibility of the ideas that lie behind healing.

Not only is there the mystery of the healer to

consider, but the very mystery of the rituals they perform. The allure of the church is based on the glamour of mystical rituals that, to be successful, require a kind of blind acquiescence from the follower. Once this is questioned, the entire edifice must collapse. This is analogous to the work of the faith healer, who also relies on a speechless complicity in his or her strange practices. If this is not there, the healer's work is all the more harder.

He or she is also the counsellor – the witch doctor. Healers offer sustenance where there has only been a counsel of despair from a doctor. This may not sound too grandiose a claim for healing, but one can easily imagine the effect of having someone tell you that your cancer is at least treatable, if not curable, when a few sleepless days before a synthetically sympathetic doctor has regaled you with the cheery news that there is no hope for you and you may as well submit placidly like a drugged factory animal to your unlovely fate. Hope itself has a curative power that cannot be overlooked, as it lessens one's symptoms and enlarges the pain threshold. Healers can be both Jesus himself and the slightly frightening figure that links us to the pagan past. Just as symbolism can work only if it bypasses the conscious mind and goes to the unconscious, the power of faith healing is all the stronger if the recipient is only dimly aware of what the healer represents.

Theatre

An element of theatre also augments the attraction of the faith healer. This is especially pronounced in American evangelists, who perhaps use the sense of the dramatic to a level where it becomes crass and tawdry, yet executed properly by a healer this can be utilised to add to his or her potency. Christ himself had a pronounced sense of theatre, exhibited in his organisation of the triumphal entry into Jerusalem and the Last Supper and, indeed, the dramatic nature of his many healings.

It is easily conceivable that for someone who has been bedridden for ten years, the very prospect of a trip to visit a faith healer could discharge recuperative agents into the metabolism, just as Mary Baker began to feel better before her meeting with Phineas Quimby. And once in the presence of the faith healer, it is hard to maintain your critical faculties when you are surrounded by de-

vout, friendly and well-meaning believers – to
keep your head, as Kipling put it, when all about
you are losing theirs. Perhaps the very practice of
healing inherently plays to our sense of the dramatic. The knowledge that faith healers pose an
ideological challenge and danger to a profession
that has become so arrogant as to be totalitarian
sets up a sense of dramatic conflict, but more than
this, the dramatic defeat of illness by a healer is a
Manichean battle between dark and light, and in-
tensely appealing.

It is ironic that the very herd instinct that doctors are wont to follow in pursuit of their profession and that so disables and detracts from that
very profession is the same herd instinct that con-
tributes so much to the success of the healing
process in the complementary sphere. A large
contributory factor to the patient's first considering the possibility of visiting a healer will be the
proximity of friends and relations who have visited a healer in the past and found it beneficial,
and who will advocate it as a possible avenue.

It is interesting to note that a large part of the attraction of complementary health therapies to the
general public resides in the glamour it is given

by the interest that the British royal family has shown in complementary health treatments. For several generations they have had a homoeopathic doctor, and, during his term as President of the BMA, Prince Charles extolled the benefits of holistic medicine, most notably in the speech he made to the BMA in 1983.

Chapter 10

Orthodox Medicine and Healing

> Your long Latin words are unable to cure
> This sickening sadness I have to endure
> So from my sorrow one thing is sure;
> Doctors, your learning is simply absurd.
>
> (Molière)

It was in the middle of the nineteenth century that science began stumblingly and slowly to approach an explanation for the occurrence of disease, and to effectively begin to thwart it. Medical treatment became constantly more effective. During the last twenty years breathtaking strides have taken place. The infant mortality rate has dropped, antibiotics cure once lethal diseases with exciting adroitness. Surgery has advanced to a startling degree. People are living longer and welcome a more easeful old age.

Our maturing comprehension of the workings of the human body, and of the troubles that harry it, give optimism that one by one the ailments that hurt it will cede to scientific medicine. Yet despite all this, gigantic areas remain where our medical knowledge remains skeletal. Patients still yield to strange contagions, to tumours and to premature failure of vital organs, when neither drugs nor surgery are effectual.

It is at times like these that people, confronted with the diagnosis of an inoperable tumour or a debilitating disease of the nervous system, such as disseminated sclerosis, decide to turn elsewhere for an answer. They may turn to faith healing, to quack remedies or pilgrimages to religious shrines. As far as one can tell from the available evidence, these actions are essayed as a last resort, and usually achieve no more than a fleeting and short-lived lift of the spirits, or the consolation of religious faith in the face of the unfair.

Yet occasionally cures do occur that correspond

with the sufferer's call to a shrine or a faith healer. There is much written evidence to this effect, which suggests that these sudden and dramatic cures are not quackery but evidence of some healing power as yet unexplained by medical science. Some of these cures are even backed up by medical evidence from qualified doctors.

For both the church and the medical profession, healing is the mad woman in the attic, the close relative that they would prefer not to talk about. But so-called 'orthodox' medicine (note the connotations of this term) is a fleeting parvenu when compared to the longevity of healing. Faith healing held sway for a full eighteen centuries, from the time before Christ when the oracle at Delphi accepted the healing powers of Asclepius up to the Renaissance and beyond to the present. It is very likely that healing is as old as mankind itself.

Beyond the Graeco-Roman world, belief in healing cures was even more common. The Persians considered the spell the most valid and trustworthy form of treatment. We should also consider the Indic culture of the East in our study. At the time from 100 to 1000 BC, the time of the Buddha and the Krishna, we find claims for magical cures alongside the use of herbal remedies. In this philosophy the *prana*, or 'life force', of yoga is equated with the healing force. Indian texts tell how this energy can be transferred by touch and through the mind for therapeutic purposes. Reports are also given of the chakras, the circular energy fields by which energy flows from the etheric to the physical body.

The sphere of orthodox medicine has at its foundation figures such as Empodocles, Hippocrates, Paracelsus, Galen (who took the cure at Pergamum, the temple erected in honour of a healing cult) and Robert Boyle (the father of modern chemistry). These were figures who were willing to attach credence to the so-called 'forgotten art'. Were all these people duped? Or were they open to something we are wilfully blind to? The symbol of medicine itself, the snake, is a symbol that arose from a story connected to Asclepius, the Greek god of healing.

The career of the faith healer follows an archetypal pattern. After a halting and tentative beginning, the healer will begin to build up a following. His or her popularity spreads and then reaches its critical mass, where he or she becomes important enough to be seen as a potential threat, as a rival power bloc, to the monopoly of the church or the medical establishment. Often the healer will have a powerful patron, but this is not enough to prevent either the physical or psychological destruction meted out to them. It is often forgotten that faith healers themselves are as much in need of positive reinforcement as their patients. A prosaic explanation will be produced by the orthodoxy in an attempt to besmirch and undermine the healer. The healer retires into seclusion, if he or she is lucky. If unlucky, he or she may end up in prison.

Sounds familiar? It should, because this is the story of virtually all faith healers, from Greatrakes to Jacob, from Rasputin to Arigo. This is a story that will be repeated until medicine begins to accept the sphere of faith healing as a legitimate branch of medicine.

In the pantheon of faith healing since the thirteenth century this pattern is endlessly repeated. Older (and wiser?) traditions extolled the healer as a functionary worthy of respect. In the case of Asclepius, the healer was a god. Yet now in America non-medical treatment is illegal in every state. How did such a falling-off occur? We have

seen how the church itself contributed to the
marginalisation of faith healing, now it is time to
call orthodox medicine to the dock.

It has become a commonplace in literature on
healing to berate the indifference of orthodox
medicine to healing and to turn members of the
medical profession into bogeymen. In some cases
this attitude is understandable, but the way forward must surely lie in dispensing with this mutual antagonism and bringing these two branches
of medicine together. Bridging this chasm would
be no mean feat, as it has been reinforced by centuries of mutual suspicion.

It is not doctors we should castigate but the system that allows them to emerge from medical
schools with a mechanistic view of human illness.
Medicine sees injury in a mechanistic way, studying the biochemical changes that are triggered in
the immune system, and how the body naturally
dams the flow of blood that is produced. While
these processes are magical and amazing enough
in themselves, the important question is the one
that addresses the interaction and influence of the
mind upon these physical processes.

The system perpetuates itself by means of a subtle (and therefore incredibly powerful) form of indoctrination. Young idealistic doctors are trained with methods stressing efficiency. They learn to treat patients no doubt as they themselves were treated and as their superiors, whom they try to imitate, treat patients. When dealing with a sick individual, the notion that one should be intuitive should never be lost sight of; otherwise we are simply 'block-booking' and forgetting that we are dealing with an individual. It is all too often the case with conventional medicine that the doctor will attempt to diminish the significance of the personal quirks of the patient to the illness in question. In contrast, the complementary practitioner sees these peculiarities as keys to the illness and the root of the cure for it. Medical students are as yet untrained in counselling skills or even rudimentary social skills.

The resentment of the spokespeople for conventional medicine is aggravated by the fact that they feel they are being undermined by people with no training in medicine. This in turn leads to resentment from the side-lined practitioners of complementary medicine, who are then driven into a more extreme position brought about by their own defensiveness. The schism between orthodox medicine and unorthodox is a corrosive one and one that is ultimately pointless. In this book I have favoured the term 'complementary medicine' over the term 'alternative medicine' as I do not wish to suggest that orthodox medicine and healing are mutually exclusive, although one could be forgiven for thinking they were.

Healers are caught in a Catch-22 situation. People with healing gifts are alienated from the church and thus tend to work in fringe religious groups, which is the precise reason they are regarded with suspicion by many Christians.

The cures that were discovered by folk medicine have now been adopted and assimilated into standard everyday medical practice. Yet the wisdom that faith healing has to offer has not made the transition into orthodoxy as yet and, apart from a few pockets of enlightenment, stands in a medicinal no-man's-land. The reasons for this are cultural and religious.

The influence of René Descartes (1596–1650), the great philosopher and mathematician who is credited with beginning modern philosophy, led to a firm dichotomising of mind and body.

Descartes believed that all animal behaviour and internal processes could be explained mechanically. On the relationship between mind and body, Descartes was a dualist, believing the two to be separate. The type of dualism he advocated was interactionism – he believed in a separate but interacting mind and body. After Descartes, some philosophers elaborated the mechanical side of his philosophy by proposing that humans were nothing but machines and the concept of mind was unnecessary.

While the influence of Cartesian ideas led us out of the Dark Ages in the physical sciences, making medicine search out physical causes for illness, these ideas were corrosive in that they denied the mind as a causal influence on the body. They led science to denigrate everything that was not explainable by theory. As well as the Cartesian outlook, the influence of the Industrial Revolution, contemporary with the prominence of Descartes, led to a growing confidence in humankind as regards the ability to master the environment. This instilled a materialistic outlook on the world, which manifested itself in an increasing emphasis on the purely physical aspects of illness. It spawned the identification of parasites, bacteria, viruses, vitamins, hormones and genetic anomalies, as well as the benefit of using chemicals to treat disease. Alexander Fleming discovered penicillin; digitalis was discovered from an old folk remedy; the physician became confident that the eradication of disease was on the horizon. Lister made innovations with the antiseptic treatment of wounds. While, of course, this is all laudable, it encouraged the practitioners of medicine to downgrade the importance of the patient's mental attitude to illness in favour of a purely physical account. It was into this gap that sects such as Christian Science leapt, filling the vacuum left when medicine became materialistic. The very word 'disease' demonstrates an awareness of the root of many illnesses – a state of absence of ease, of psychological tranquillity, yet this was a reasoning that passed by many in the medical profession. The term 'shell-shock' from the First World War was a manifestation of the unwillingness of conventional medicine to accept that war left psychological damage as well as physical. The disjunction of physical and psychological approaches to healing has prevailed from antiquity.

Egyptian papyri delineate two wings of therapy –
one involving charms and incantations, the other
scientific approaches employing medicine.

Orthodox humanistic medicine traditionally advocated healing through regimen and diet, contrary to the claim of the complementary health
fraternity that they were the authors of the holistic
approach to therapy. The problem lies in the
medical fraternity's apparent unwillingness to act
on this knowledge. Doctors have known for years
that what goes on in a patient's mind is as important as the biochemical processes within the body.
At the beginning of the nineteenth century,
Johann Heinroth, a German clergyman, invented
the word 'psychosomatic', which unites two
words meaning 'mind' and 'body' and emphasises that a sick person can be cured only when his
or her psychological make-up is considered as
well as the disturbed organs. There are specific
kinds of illness in which the state of the patient's
mental attitude to the malady is of primary importance to the success or failure of its management.
It is perhaps more than pure coincidence that
these are the illnesses in which faith healing has
much of its success.

The first and most obvious of these are afflictions that can be of a psychosomatic character, such as headaches, vomiting and rashes. Another branch are illnesses that are short lasting and which the body's normal mechanisms will combat in due time. These include muscular aches and pains, and even warts. With these illnesses a positive mental attitude is as important as the physical cure. A further category is terminal illnesses, where there will be great fluctuations in progress as the disease moves towards its inevitable conclusion.

This knowledge, however, was ignored for a great interval of time as the discovery of the germs that caused diseases such as tuberculosis, cholera and syphilis persuaded doctors that every illness was the result of a specific germ. If they could isolate the germ, they could confidently cure the disease with drugs or by other physical means. They ignored the effects of mental experiences on the progress of disease and treated the body as a machine.

The term 'psychosomatic' is still used in a pejorative sense by doctors, with the faintly patronising and dismissive implication that the patient is being soft and weak-willed. It has been estimated that illnesses involving a psychosomatic factor apply to some 80 per cent of diseases. As regards faith healing, one can either view this fact negatively or positively. One can say that this proves the validity and appropriateness of faith healing to deal with the kinds of illness that consume and plague the mind. Conversely, one could say that this fact demonstrates that faith healing's success can be placed in the realm of primitive psychiatry and its triumphs can be put down to suggestion rather than a divinity shaping our ends.

The limits of orthodox medicine

In fairness to conventional medicine, it is clear that we often overestimate the abilities of the medical profession. People still surrender to inexplicable viral infections, to tumours, and to premature failure of vital organs, when drugs or surgery are less than useless. Orthodox medicine has failed to provide cures for a whole array of conditions, including Aids, arthritis, cancer and heart disease. The physician or surgeon does not cure disease; he or she only assists the natural processes of cure, which are performed by the intrinsic healing and renewing ability of the human body. The English physician Thomas Sydenham wrote: 'I often think more could be left to nature than we are in the habit of leaving to her; to imagine that she always wants the help of art is an error, and an unlearned error too.'

We should remember that many mechanistic medical treatments, such as chemotherapy and radiation therapy for cancer, are toxic and deleterious and may even be of unproven value. Until recently electroconvulsive therapy was employed by the medical profession, albeit as a last resort.

Robert Buckmann reports that only fifteen per cent of medical practice can be said to be based on 'sound science'. As for the rest, the doctor will employ the very things that a healer will – that is, an amalgam of folklore, individual predilection and observation.

Many New Age commentators are often to be found bewailing the exclusivity of the orthodox medical establishment and the willingness they (whoever 'they' are) display to dismiss complementary medicine. Yet often what seems to lie behind this is a desire amongst the New-Agers to paint themselves as romantic outsiders excluded by the orthodoxy. The truth of the matter is that in some areas of medicine there is a great receptivity to complementary medicine. Oncologists (those who study tumours) have always displayed a holistic approach to medicine. Furthermore, meditation and dietary manipulation may be considered complementary to orthodox, proved therapies. What is needed as we enter the next millennium is a synthesis between the wisdom of faith healing and conventional medicine. At this point holistic medicine as a mainstream idea is in its childhood. Several of the leading exponents in this new area of medicine acknowledge healing as a holistic regimen.

A Devon GP, Michael Dixon, has been referring many of his patients to the faith healer Gill White for over three years. Initially, his fellow doctors in practice were sceptical but eventually they became receptive to the idea once the results became evident.

Dr Dixon used the first fifty of his patients who had seen the healer to conduct an enquiry into the success of the referral. These results were published in *Connection*, the membership journal of the Royal College of General Practitioners. Seventy-five per cent said that their symptoms were 'much better' and 30 per cent said they were 'very much better'. The success of the healer was so impressive that Dr Dixon is now funded by the Family Health Services Authority in researching the effects of healing, and a second healer has been taken on. Interestingly, the ailments that seem to respond to treatment more readily are arthritis, eczema, back pain, stress and depression.

What this illustrates is that we cannot generalise about the receptivity of orthodox medicine to what healing has to offer. As long as there are men with the open-minded-ness and vision of Michael Dixon, it is unfair to defame the medical profession for its narrow-mindedness towards complementary medicine. Particular branches, such as oncology, will be more receptive than others to what healing has to offer.

Perhaps the increasing receptivity of the medical profession towards complementary medicine is born not of a healthy intellectual openness but of desperation in the face of its own failure to combat a growing number of illnesses that conventional medicine is impotent against.

One should always be mindful of the propensity

for advances in medical knowledge to come from the most unlikely quarters. The old wives' cure for a wound entailed binding it in cobwebs. Cobwebs, we now know, are rich in penicillin. Who are we to say that the practice of faith healing does not contain some hidden truth as yet unreachable by the current grasp of medicine?

The limits of our understanding

We rely on direct demonstration of the curative value of a treatment to believe in the efficacy of a particular therapy. This relies on the availability of a viable method by which we can test the claim. In some cases, however, this simply does not exist. For example, the Ancient Romans knew that disease within the arteries caused angina. Yet verification of this knowledge was only really available in the 1930s, when Werner Forsmann put a catheter into his own heart finally to prove the truth of this assertion.

It is quite possible that a relevant test of what precisely happens during the healing process is not yet available to us, and as yet it is simply inappropriate to dismiss it as a form of therapy. It may be premature to perform experiments on healing without first knowing the essence of the processes that take place. Not knowing the very nature of these processes may bias what is found.

It is conceivable that there might be an aptitude in humankind to cure, which is reliant on some dimly understood emanation that is now an enigma to humanity. It may be that, in terms of getting near to a fuller understanding of precisely what is happening when a healer cures, we are like a caveman trying to comprehend chaos theory. An element of suggestion is assuredly a factor in these healings, but this falls woefully short of explaining the cures. Whatever the inter-action that occurs between healer and patient – presupposing that there is one – no one has as yet offered any definitive explanation of what it might be composed.

We should remind ourselves that what is today regarded as pseudo-science may in the future be-come part of medical practice, and one can never be entirely certain that one is right to dismiss new claims. It is quite possible that there might be an ability in humans to heal, which is not the doing of a deity or a devil but accountable to some mys-terious force, as yet unexplained or unexplainable with the current vocabulary of medical science. An article in *New Scientist* magazine in 1995 bewailed the fact that we are not prepared to discuss the extent of what we simply do not know. Instead we swagger and preen and talk complacently of what we do understand.

It is important to consider the idea that the beneficial aspects of having visited a healer do not easily lend themselves to being quantified in a scientific way. After you have seen a healer or a healing doctor, you may behave slightly differently, and people may perceive you differently, leading to a chain of positive effects that bolsters your sense of wellbeing, reducing your symptoms and increasing your pain threshold. These are all very subtle changes, and changes that we ourselves may not even be consciously aware of.

This means examining the psychological, cultural and social aspects of illness and health, and the importance of understanding not only the means by which a patient's physical system comes to work properly but also the way in which the patient comes to feel well again and is re-integrated into his or her society as a full participant.

There is a detectable shift in some medical quarters at least from placing the emphasis on relieving symptoms and curing disease to the broader question of how healing itself occurs. What we need, as we enter the next millennium, is a synthesis between the wisdom of faith healing and conventional medicine. Just as the nature-nurture debate can be resolved only by the bringing together of sociology and socio-biology, so too can medicine proceed only when it comes to some meaningful rapprochement with healing and the rest of complementary medicine. We should denigrate neither conventional medicine nor healing but begin the peace process between the two in the spirit of human enterprise.

The Healing Goes On . . .

The debate about the validity of faith healing will continue, as will the battle between scientific empiricism and age-old mysticism. It may be fatuous to argue the case for a subject that is dimly understood and of which, moreover, there can be no one authoritative definition.

It does, however, seem churlish to question the validity of anything that eases suffering, even if that relief is branded as imaginary. Are we really so confused and deluded that we do not know how we feel, and, if so, is it really so bad to make someone believe that they feel better?

At a recent alternative health exhibition in Glasgow, the authors spoke to a friendly and helpful woman who was fronting the stall for 'spiritual healing'. This was no crank, but an ordinary human being with an open mind and a curiosity into the faith healing phenomenon. What was especially heartening was her willingness to express her doubts and worries about the subject; some of the religious groups that she had had attachments with had been too doctrinal, too intent upon making every one of their followers think the same. She confessed that she did not truly understand what powers were at work when her healer colleagues used their skills, but that the results spoke for themselves.

And there it is; however mired in quackery we may believe it to be, and however contrary to our beliefs, we have to accept faith healing if it can relieve just one ounce of pain in one individual.

Indeed, the one thing that we can be emphatic about is the imperative of healing. Perhaps the question should not be 'Does faith healing exist?' but 'Why do we need faith healing?' It does not take long to figure out. We live in an instant culture that is fragmented and self-absorbed. Saturated with cynicism, we have declared ideology dead.

We get our reality second-hand from a flickering box, waste our faith on Saturday night lottery draws, and pay strangers to listen to our fears. Gone are the days when you went to your minister or priest for spiritual guidance. People have lost faith in the church and never had faith in the government, which is why they are turning inwards to find faith in themselves.

If, as many religions espouse, God is indeed inside every one of us, churchmen all over the world must be laughing into their cassocks. It would appear that what we thought we had rejected, we have simply re-invented and accepted in a different form.

It seems ironic that from such cultural rubble, such a bright hope has emerged. Perhaps our high-rise existence has brought us closer to God. Or perhaps the higher power that we long for, and sometimes feel we can sense, is in fact the sum total of our projected individual faiths. Perhaps this is the force that heals, and *all* healing is faith healing. Still, that's a lot of maybes.

One thing that is certain is that we are a sick society, and it is not hard to see that our world is itself wracked with disease and in desperate need of healing. War, poverty and pollution are the earth's equivalent of anger, despair and anxiety, and are ravaging the planet in the same devastating ways in which these emotions affect our bodies. Indeed, perhaps these global 'illnesses' are manifestations of our own sickness as we project our accumulated rage and fear out into the wider environment.

Each individual is a microcosm of the universe, and the way towards a healthy planet lies in healing ourselves and each other. Through healing ourselves we heal the world, and vice-versa, and the first step towards self-healing is self-love.

So as we limp into the next millennium, a message has to be sent around the world – a message of positivity and love. Love that has the power to heal.

Further Reading

Ashe, Geoffrey *Miracles* Routledge & Kegan Paul Ltd 1978

Booth Howard *Healing Experiences* Bible Reading Fellowship 1985

Brennan J. H. *Occult Reich* Futura Books 1974

Buckley, J. M. *What is the New Age?* Hodder and Stoughton 1990

Buckley, Michael *Christian Healing* CTS Publications 1990

Buckman, Robert *Magic or Medicine?* Channel Four Books 1993

Butterworth, John *Cults and New Faiths* Lion 1981

Cornwell, John *Powers of Darkness, Powers of Light* Viking/Penguin Books Ltd 1991

De Jonge, Alex *Grigori Rasputin* Collins 1982

Eddy, M.B.G. *Science and Health* Boston 1875

Gerson, Scott *Ayurveda* Element books 1993

Gordon, Stuart *The Paranormal* Headline Books.1992

Grills, Joan *Life of Christ* Oxford University Press 1984

Haggard, H.W. *Devils, Drugs and Doctors* Heinemann, n.d.

Harper, Michael *Healings of Jesus* The Jesus library 1986

Harvey, David *The Power to Heal* Aquarian 1983

Hergenhahn, B.R. *History of Psychology* Wadsworth 1986

Herzberg, Eileen *Healing* Thorsons 1988

Hodgkinson, Liz *Spiritual Healing* Piatkus 1990

Jackson, Edgar *The Role of Faith in Healing* SCM 1981

Kelsey, Morton *Healing and Christianity* SCM 1973

Kennet, Frances *Folk Medicine* Marshall Cavendish 1984

Kroll, Una *In Touch with Healing* BBC 1986

Ahmed, Rollo *The Black Art* Arrow books 1966

Large, John Ellis *The Ministry of Healing* Purnell and Sons 1959

MacNutt, Francis *Healing* Ave Maria Press 1974

MacNutt, Francis *The Power to Heal* Ave Maria Press 1977

Major, R.H. *Faiths that Healed* New York, 1940

Maple, Eric *The Dark World of Witches* Pan books 1962

Marnham, Patrick *Lourdes – A Modern Pilgrimage* Heinemann, 1980.

Meel, George *Healers and the Healing Process* Quest books 1977

Nash, Wanda *At Ease with Stress* Longman and Todd 1984

Nataf, Andre *Dictionary of the Occult* Wordsworth 1991

Neame, Alan *Lourdes* Viking/Penguin Books Ltd, 1991

O'Neil, Andrew *Charismatic Healing* The Mercier Press 1988

Parsons, Stephen *The Challenge of Christian Healing* WBC Print 1986

Peel, Robert *Spiritual Healing in a Scientific Age* Harper and Row 1987

Pitts, J *Divine Healing – Fact and Fiction* Arthur James 1962

Randi, James *The Faith Healers* Prometheus books 1987

Ritchie, Jean *The Secret World of Cults* Harper Collins 1992

Rose, Louis *Faith Healing* Penguin Books 1968

Sanford, Agnes *Healing Gifts of the Spirit* Arthur James n.d

Sanford, Agnes *The Healing Light* Arthur James n.d.

Shaykh, Fadhlalla Haeri *Elements of Sufism* Element books 1990

Shiels, W. J. *The Church and Healing* Blackwell 1982

Shine, Betty *Mind to Mind* Bantam 1989

Singer, Charles *From Magic to Science* Ernest Benn 1928

Speck, Peter *Loss and Grief in Medicine* Bailliere Tindall 1978

Stevens, Anthony *On Jung* Routledge 1990

Taylor, Allegra *Healing Hands* MacDonald Optima 1992

Vitebsky, Piers *The Shaman* DBP 1995

Werfel, Franz *The Song of Bernadette* Mayflower Books Ltd, 1977

Wimber, John *Power Healing* Hodder and Stoughton 1986

Useful Addresses

Acorn Christian Healing Trust
Whitehill Chase
High Street
Bordon
Hampshire GU35 OAP
Tel: 01420 478 121/472 779

Ayurvedic Medicine and Transcendental Meditation
Freepost
London SWlP 4YY
Tel: 0990 143 733

British Association for Counselling
1 Regent Place
Rugby
Warwickshire CV21 2PJ
Tel: 01788 578 328

College of Psychic Studies
16 Queensberry Place
London SW7 2EB
Tel: 0171 589 3292/3

Centre for Alternative Education and Research
Rosemerryn
Lamorna
Penzance
Cornwall TR19 6BN
Tel: 01736 810 530

Confederation of Healing Organisations
(contact and distant healing)
Suite J
113 High Street
Berkhamsted
Hertfordshire BP4 2DJ
Tel: 01442 870 660

Eagle's Wing Centre for Contemporary Shamanism
58 Westbere Road
London NW2 3RU
Tel: 0171 435 8174

Council for Complementary
and Alternative Medicine
Park Terrace
206-208 Latimer Road
London W10 6RE
Tel: 0181 968 3862

The Institute for Complementary Medicine
19a Portland Place
London WlM 9AD

The National Federation of
Spiritual Healers (NFSH)
Old Manor Farm Studio
Church Street
Sunbury-on-Thames
Middlesex TW16 6RJ
Tel: 01932 783 164/5

The Radionic Association
Baerlein House
Goose Green
Deddington
Oxfordshire OX15 0SZ
Tel: 01869 338 852

The Shiatsu Society
Suite D
Barbar House
Storey's Bar Road
Fengate
Peterborough PE1 5YS
Tel: 01733 758 341

Soul Directed Astrology
5a Cedar Road
Sutton, Surrey SM2 5DA
Tel: 0181 643 4898

Spiritualist Association of
Great Britain
33 Belgrave Square
London SWlX 8QB
Tel: 0171 235 3351

Alternatives
St James Centre for Health and
Healing
197 Piccadilly
London WlV 9LS
Tel: 0171 287 6711

Westbank Natural Health
Centre
Stathmiglo
Cupar
Fife
Scotland KY14 7QP
Tel: 01337 860 233

The Association of Natural
Medicine
27 Braintree Road
Witham
Essex CM8 2BS
Tel: 01376 502 762

Matthew Manning Healing
Centre
P.O. Box 100
Bury St Edmund's
Suffolk IP29 4DE
Tel: 01284 830 222

New Zealand Federation of
Spiritual Healers
P.O. Box 9502
Newmarket
Auckland
New Zealand

Outside UK

The Australian Spiritual Heal-
ers' Association
P.O. Box 4073
8 Mile Plains
Queensland 4113
Australia